SCHIZO...

and C...

D0505118

ABOUT THE AUTHORS:

Dr J. C. Cutting, MD, FRCP, FRCPsych, M Phil, trained at Guy's Hospital, London, and then worked as a general physician and neurologist before taking up a career in psychiatry. He specializes in the treatment of schizophrenia and worked at the Maudsley and Bethlem Royal Hospitals in south London from 1973 to 1993. He is now attached to the Institute of Psychiatry. Dr Cutting has written scientific papers on schizophrenia and related subjects and is the author of *The Psychology of Schizophrenia* (Churchill Livingstone, 1985) and, with Professor Michael Shepherd, *The Clinical Roots of the Schizophrenia Concept* (Cambridge University Press, 1987). A third book, *The Right Cerebral Hemisphere and Psychiatric Disorders* was published by Oxford University Press in 1990. Dr Cutting is now preparing *Two Worlds, Two Minds, Two Hemispheres* for publication by OUP in 1996.

Anne Charlish is the author of 20 books, including *Birth-Tech: Tests and Technology in Pregnancy and Birth*, *Smoking*, and *Losing Weight Naturally*. She won the Medical Journalists' Association Pain Relief Award (1993) for her *Complete Arthritis Handbook*. She broadcasts and contributes regularly to magazines, including *Essentials*, *Good Housekeeping* and *Health & Fitness*.

SCHIZOPHRENIA

UNDERSTANDING AND COPING WITH THE ILLNESS

Dr John Cutting and Anne Charlish

Thorsons
An Imprint of HarperCollins*Publishers*

Thorsons
An Imprint of HarperCollins*Publishers*
77–85 Fulham Palace Road,
Hammersmith, London W6 8JB

1160 Battery Street,
San Francisco, California 94111–1213

Published by Thorsons 1995
1 3 5 7 9 10 8 6 4 2

A catalogue record for this book
is available from the British Library

ISBN 0 7225 3122 2

Printed in Great Britain by
HarperCollinsManufacturing Glasgow

CONTENTS

INTRODUCTION

Schizophrenia is a severely disabling and disruptive illness in which part of the mind ceases to function properly. This causes the person suffering with schizophrenia to experience and think about the world and themselves in a totally different way from the rest of us. They completely lose touch with reality.

Schizophrenia is common, affecting 1 in 100 people at some time in their lives. It is also very mysterious in the behaviour it produces, alternating between periods of apparent normality and bouts of disturbance. On the positive side, however, most cases can be effectively treated. For this reason it is crucial to make the correct diagnosis at an early stage. Treatment is more likely to succeed if the illness is treated early. If misdiagnosed the schizophrenia can persist untreated for years, and consequently may gradually worsen.

Drug treatment is a thorny issue, and this I have dealt with in Chapter 6. The first problem concerns the reluctance of a number of schizophrenics to take medication; the second is the dosage of the drugs. The two problems are interlinked in that *most* of the drugs cause unwanted side-effects in *some* patients; however, not all of the available drugs cause side-effects in all patients. It is a matter, therefore, of trial and error in finding the drug that suits the patient and thus avoiding the possibility that the patient may refuse treatment altogether.

The second aspect of the problem is that many doctors, psychiatrists and general practitioners alike prescribe either too little, or more commonly too much of a drug. Every drug has a level at which it works, known as the therapeutic dose (meaning, literally, the helping dose). If you take too little it won't work. If you take too much the side-effects will outweigh whatever good the drug is producing. If side-effects persist when the dose is reduced to its lowest therapeutic level, then the possibility of trying another drug should be discussed with the consultant. After all, there are over a dozen drugs that can be prescribed for schizophrenia. For these reasons I have described in some detail the available drugs, together with a note of their therapeutic dose.

In my practice as a Consultant Psychiatrist in the National Health Service, I see some 200 people with schizophrenia each year, sometimes with their relatives. Some are referred to me by their local psychiatrist, others are referred from all over the country. I have written this book to help sufferers and their families and friends cope with what is, without doubt, a devastating illness.

Understanding the nature of a problem often helps to understand its manifestations. It is just as important, however, to try to understand what a person who has schizophrenia is going through. The experiences of some schizophrenics are described in Chapter 1. Chapter 2 discusses what schizophrenia is (and what it is not). How schizophrenia can be recognized is described in Chapter 3. Just who is at risk of developing schizophrenia is the subject of Chapter 4, while Chapter 5 explores the possible causes of schizophrenia. Chapter 6 deals with the complex question of treatment. Chapters 7 and

8 will, I hope, be of special help and reassurance to people with schizophrenia and their family and friends.

Most people with schizophrenia – over two-thirds – will recover satisfactorily from their first episode of the illness with treatment. If they remain on medication, and this may have to be for the rest of their lives, they will stay out of hospital and be able to lead independent lives. This is a marked change from the time before effective drugs were discovered (the 1950s), when two-thirds or even three-quarters of all schizophrenics had to stay in mental hospitals for the rest of their lives.

My hope is that my research and this book may help all those who suffer with schizophrenia, as well as those who have a schizophrenic sufferer in the family, and that we may one day see the early diagnosis and effective treatment of all patients.

Dr John Cutting
Consultant Psychiatrist
Sussex, 1995

1

EXPERIENCING SCHIZOPHRENIA

Some 30 million people worldwide (600,000 in Britain) know what it is like to experience the mental chaos characterized by schizophrenia. Margaret, a sufferer, describes here what a schizophrenic breakdown was like for her, at the time of her first illness many years ago, when she was 23:

> Things just slipped out of my grasp. It was unsteady relationships. I got worked up. All of a sudden things slipped out of my grasp. I couldn't hold my thoughts. Especially the reasoning process. I saw everything in abstract terms, a void. But that was basically to do with unsteady relationships. And also, both times it was spurred on by other people. Always some kind of emotion, a shock experience to the system. I'd put my faith in a friend and I was then let down. Then things went out of my grasp. Then after that I couldn't keep hold of my thoughts. My mind was wandering all over the place. I couldn't keep it together.

Some people with schizophrenia hear voices, some say that they are commanded by invisible forces to do or say things that seem strange to the rest of us; others find that they see, hear or smell everyday things in an unusual and bizarre way. A few believe that they have turned into someone or something else, such as Jesus, the heir to some royal throne, or a monkey. Schizophrenia, then, means something different for each individual. This is not surprising when you consider that everyone experiences events and sensations in an individual way; each of us has highly individual thoughts, feelings and experiences even when we are well. In mental illness, including schizophrenia, such individuality naturally still exists. In this respect, mental illness is quite unlike physical illness in which signs and symptoms are less marked by individual variation and therefore more straightforward to describe and diagnose.

Compare now Margaret's description of what she was thinking with this account, given by Peter, who also had his first breakdown in his twenties:

> There was a tremendous feeling of claustrophobia, of being trapped. Traffic was too loud. Too many people on the pavement. Walls were moving in on me. I'd panic that the house was getting too small. Then I'd go outside. But outside the noise was too great. Nowhere, nowhere I could cope. Not even safe in bed ... All the bright colours frightened me most, orange and red ... I recognized people everywhere ... I had all these thoughts in my head but when I spoke it was just noise, just high-pitched noises came out. It had lost the meaning. I could understand other people's language but not my own.

Fundamental Features of Schizophrenia

The experience of schizophrenia differs greatly from person to person, but there are, nevertheless, two fundamental features of the illness: a disturbance in *thinking* (usually referred to as thought disorder) and a disturbance in how the world is seen, a disturbance in *perception* (usually known as perceptual disorder). If you read Margaret's account again, you will see that she is describing her thoughts and the workings of her mind rather than what she sees around her. Peter, on the other hand, shows disturbances in his perception of the world: he talks about the traffic being too loud, the house seeming too small, frightening colours and noises.

Both Margaret's and Peter's accounts describe a psychotic experience, their experience of psychosis. Psychosis means any form of severe mental disorder in which the individual's contact with reality becomes severely distorted. A psychotic person's perceptions and thoughts about the world are no longer within the normal range of experience. Their reality is no longer our reality. Schizophrenia is a psychosis that is characterized by a particular disorder of perception and thinking. (What schizophrenia is – and what it is not – are described more fully in Chapter 2.)

Both Margaret and Peter gave their accounts of the first few days of their schizophrenic breakdown many years after the experience. (Both are now well.) Margaret's description reflects very clearly what the first stage of a breakdown is like. She is struggling with her thoughts, trying to get them in order, but they elude her and she loses control. She puts the blame on events happening around her, but this probably reflects a natural tendency of the human mind to seek causes for disordered mental functioning in one's environment.

For Peter it was the world around him that appeared different. His perception was affected. Sounds, things that he saw, even his own voice and the words that he spoke had all changed.

Delusions and Hallucinations

As days turn into weeks, thought disorder and perceptual disorder become more firmly entrenched and both can give rise to delusions, which are false *beliefs* about the world, and hallucinations, which are false *perceptions* with no basis in reality.

Susan, in the third day of her breakdown, had already started to develop delusions:

> Yesterday I thought it was the end of the world. Everlasting night. I thought the atom bomb was going to be dropped. Walking along I seemed to be walking on the spot. I didn't seem to be getting anywhere. Fog seemed to be thicker down roads where I shouldn't go than roads where I should go. Some weird thing was telling me I was Jesus Christ. I didn't want to be. I just wanted to be a whore. It's difficult to think. My thoughts seem to turn to stone ... my thoughts appear above my head in a bubble.

Martin, in his second week of a breakdown, described his experiences like this:

> I heard a voice. It said 'He's getting things the wrong way.' While I was walking along the street it said 'He's walking, you know.' Then it said 'He's not moving.' Then, when I was sitting quietly there were two voices. One, a male voice, said 'I can't get anything out of him.' The other, a female, said 'He can actually hear us.'

Both Susan and Martin were at the height of their schizophrenic breakdown when they gave these accounts. Susan had begun to interpret her abnormal perceptual experiences in bizarre ways, for instance into a belief that she was Jesus Christ. This new belief is an example of delusion. Martin's abnormal perceptual experiences now took the form of clear-cut voices commenting on his actions. Hearing voices is probably the best-known symptom of schizophrenia: an hallucination of sound (known, therefore, as auditory hallucinations). Vincent Van Gogh, one of the world's greatest artists, is thought to have developed schizophrenia with auditory hallucinations; he was so troubled by the voices he persistently heard that he cut off one of his ears in an attempt to dispel them.

A New World

Disorders of thinking and perception are the fundamental features of schizophrenia and its most common manifestations. Those of us who know someone with schizophrenia can recognize these features as abnormal and peculiar in some way, as can sufferers themselves, once they have recovered. For sufferers in the middle of the illness, however, these thoughts and perceptions are reality. Their beliefs and experiences are just as real to them at that time as our own are to each of us. For the period of their illness, schizophrenics enter a new world, a world of new perceptions and new thoughts which is completely different from anything that a normal person experiences. Describing this new world and trying to tell us of their experiences is one of the greatest problems for people with schizophrenia because there is no language or adequate way of describing something that is not normally within reality.

DISTURBED THINKING

A change in the way that someone with schizophrenia thinks, combined with changes in perception, can form and maintain delusions, particularly if the sufferer is not diagnosed and treated quickly. Disturbed thinking can take various forms, and schizophrenics themselves emphasize different aspects of their thinking disorder.

As we have seen, Margaret was later able to describe how she gradually lost control of her thoughts. Raymond's thought disturbance took a different form: he had the experience of thinking in two different ways at the same time.

> *'I was functioning on another level, one more in pictures, then another one. The abnormal one was the picture one.'*

Claude felt that:

> *'Rational thinking was not right. There was my own personality and another one.'*

Some remember thinking more deeply, particularly about their past. Paul, for example:

> *'I thought much more deeply about things like the meaning of life and values. My whole world seemed to cave in. I kept thinking about my birthplace and my past.'*

Sean described vividly how his new way of thinking took over his whole life and became his entire world:

> I was lying on my bed and reality somehow passed inwards as if my brain turned round. I then became more interested in memory than perceiving reality around me. I was interested in doing things and being in places which brought out my memory rather than seeking new experiences. Perception in itself of new things I was no longer curious of. Reality became rather threatening, separate, boring. I had a sense of things being second-hand, stale, lacking freshness. I was no longer surprised by anything.

Thought disorder in schizophrenia is often more clearly revealed in a schizophrenic's writings than in his or her conversation. Not only is the *content* unusual but the *form* in which it is written may be peculiar. The grammatical construction of sentences may be wrong or bizarre, the ideas unconnected and the whole piece may read like gibberish. Psychiatrists call this *formal thought disorder* because it is the *form* of what is expressed rather than the content which is most abnormal. The same features may exist in speech, but written accounts usually demonstrate it better.

This extract was taken from the writings of one of the patients of Swiss psychiatrist Eugen Bleuler, the doctor who coined the term schizophrenia in 1911. The extract illustrates both disorder of form and disorder of content:

> At the time of the new moon Venus stands in the Augutsky of Egypt and lights up with its light rays the merchant-travel-harbours of Suez, Cairo and Alexandria. In this historically famous Caliphcity is the museum of Assyrian statues from Macedonia. Besides pisang, also corn, oats, clover and barley grow there. Bananas, figs, lemons, oranges and olives. Olive oil is an Arabian liqueur sauce which the Afghans, Blackamoors and Moslemites use for ostrich breeding.

The content is bizarre, for example, because olive oil is not an Arabian liqueur sauce and is not likely to have been used, even by the most out-of-the-way tribes, for breeding ostriches. The form is also bizarre because the patient uses completely made-up words such as Augutsky and joins together real words to make up a word which is not to be found in a dictionary, for example Caliphcity. His word Moslemite is not correct either, although its meaning is clear. All these are technically known as *neologisms* – the Greek for 'new words'. Given the unusual content, the grammar is reasonable. The train of ideas is rather devious but it is difficult to judge this, given the strange topic the patient chose to write about.

In the following example from a schizophrenic, the content is understandable but the flow of ideas shifts all the time. Alan, a man of 35, was asked how he felt:

> What I'm saying is my mother is too ill. No money. It all comes out of her pocket. My flat's leaking. It's ruined my mattress. It's Lambeth Council. I'd like to know what the caption in the motto under their coat of arms is. It's in Latin. It must mean that you've got semen in you, the spunk to do something. The other thing I'm telling you is my birth certificate. Do you remember when I was in that hospital. I was on my knees.

Each statement within its phrase is quite normal but bears little relationship to the previous one. Psychiatrists have given this feature of schizophrenic speech or writing various names, without really understanding what it represents. Emil Kraepelin, the German psychiatrist who is regarded as the father of modern psychiatry, called it *derailment*. (Kraepelin was the first psychiatrist to recognize schizophrenia, in 1896, though he called it by a different name – dementia praecox.) The term derailment is a good one in my view because it suggests a train gradually slipping off the track with the engine becoming more and more out of alignment with each successive carriage. Other psychiatrists have called it *tangentiality* because each idea is at a tangent to the preceding one; other terms for it are *loosening of associations*, and *Knight's move thinking* – because of the two-forwards-and-one-sideways move made by this piece in chess.

The grammar in a schizophrenic's writings may be so bad that any meaning is almost totally lost, as in this extract from a patient's letter:

> *Dr John*
>
> *Its Jean I have got lives left on my hands and No Help as they have Blinded John Easdeam and injected. V.D. Cut his Penace of John has spoken to Me same place where they clubised you down. where William and Cromwall are Smith Blinded John and Cut his Penace and he was the one that Blinded Peter Hindsman and they have let out his home to American People.*

The technical term for the way that Jean has expressed her thoughts in this letter is *incoherence*, although it is possible to uncover some themes. Neologism, derailment and incoherence, all illustrated above, are characteristic of schizophrenic writing and therefore of the thought disorder seen in schizophrenia.

Real Meanings

There is one other feature of schizophrenic thought disorder, witnessed both in writings and conversation, which is not so obvious until one has seen a number of different extracts from the writings of people with schizophrenia. This feature is known as a breakdown in the pragmatic or everyday use of language. In normal, everyday conversation, we use language in a variety of ways. If a boss says to a secretary, 'There are too many mistakes in this letter,' this is a fairly clear request to retype it. Yet the secretary could not know this merely by analysing the precise meaning of each word of the sentence. In the same way, we all know that if someone greets us with: 'How are you?' they do not expect us to reply literally. It is a convention, an alternative to 'Hello.' The pragmatic meaning of a piece of speech, therefore, is its meaning within the accepted rules of conversation, and not its literal meaning. If we replied every time someone said 'How are you?' with a whole list of everything that we were feeling and everything which was on our mind – 'the cat's got fleas, the roof's leaking, the kitchen's flooded, the next door neighbour's unfriendly,' etc. – we would soon be regarded as odd.

People with schizophrenia, however, frequently do take things literally when the situation calls for a metaphorical or pragmatic approach to language. John, for example, noticed the following sentence in a newspaper: 'We must all be concerned with what is right in our daily lives.' The writer obviously meant the word right to be understood in a moral sense, but John took it to mean right as opposed to left. Because of this he became concerned with the neighbour in the flat to the right of his own and came to believe that this neighbour was persecuting him. In other words, he formed a delusion because of his thought disorder.

PERCEPTUAL DISORDER

A schizophrenic's perception of the world is often so far removed from reality that it becomes very frightening for the sufferer at the height of the illness, so much so that suicide attempts are not uncommon. Denise recalls:

'Everything appeared weird. Colours were vivid. Faces were distorted. The world looked nasty and horrible. I didn't want to live in it.'

Practically everything may appear to be altered or hostile in some way, and the schizophrenic's bizarrely distorted perceptions may also affect all the senses: sight, hearing, smell, touch and taste. Marjorie, for example, experienced hallucinations in several of her senses. She thought her grandson smelled of chloroform (an olfactory hallucination), that her bed was burning hot (a tactile or touch hallucination) and that her heart was pounding and she was about to have a heart attack (a bodily or somatic hallucination). She also had abnormal sexual sensations: making love with her husband felt strange and unusually intense.

Colours are often experienced differently. Stella remembers:

'Black looked brown sometimes. Brown looked red.'

People, particularly their faces, are often distorted in shape or expression. Stella again:

'All I could see were people in cars. They looked like ghosts, they looked different as if they were statues, monuments, as if they were dead and cremated.'

Strangers may look intensely familiar or relatives look like strangers. What must be particularly upsetting is the commonly reported experience that one's own body feels strange. Fay:

'For months I couldn't look in the mirror because I resembled a devil. People kept coming up to me in the street and saying "I know you," but I didn't know them.'

Sounds may appear different and even language may lose its meaning. Linda:

'Everything sounded clearer. It seemed as if I could hear for miles. As if I could hear people down the street. I thought my language was wrong. I believed that no one could understand what I said.'

David:

'I used to get the sudden thing that I couldn't understand what people said, like it was a foreign language.'

Thomas:

> *'I seemed to have an American accent, slurry as if I were drunk but wasn't.'*

Is there any consistent pattern to these changes in the way someone with schizophrenia experiences themselves and the world around them? Many researchers have tried to find a common theme: for example, is a schizophrenic's world more vivid than ours? Or is it more unreal, as if one were watching a film? It is now known that neither of these suggestions accurately conveys the schizophrenic experience. Some people with schizophrenia remember their world as dull, so increased vividness is not the whole answer. Jane, for instance, recalls:

> *'Sometimes I would go into the firm and it looked stale. Everything was on a low ebb, muddier.'*

Although most people with schizophrenia appreciate, in retrospect, that their sense of reality did change, few describe it simply as a sense of unreality. The following comments from various sufferers emphasize this:

> *'Things were unreal, only from a mental viewpoint, not through my eyes.'*

> *'It wasn't really unreal, it was just strange, funny, different; I can't explain.'*

> *'Both I felt unreal and things around seemed extra-real.'*

> *'Real not unreal.'*

> *'Unreal and extra-real at the same time.'*

It is as if their world is so strange that normal language, derived, as it is, from human experience of the normal world, is no longer adequate. If anything, the change appears to involve not so much how things are in themselves (for example, a cow still looks like a cow always did) but how things relate to each other. It is the overall scene that looks odd, not the individual items that make it up. Desmond tried hard to put his experiences across to me:

> I couldn't recognize any of my surroundings – people, places ... it was a general lack of orientation. I could recognize certain things. I could recognize qualities of a place, qualities of surfaces. It was the organization of things which was different. Things didn't actually look different in themselves.

Even colours weren't actually different for Desmond:

> *'There was some change, a certain shine, not really a change in colour.'*

The most striking change that many sufferers from schizophrenia observe is how individual things in the environment seem to stand out from their background. Mary:

> *'Obstacles, chairs, buildings took on a life of their own. These inanimate objects seemed to become alive and be making threatening gestures.'*

Sarah, an art student, remembers:

> *'It was like being in one of my paintings. I used to go outside and look at the houses with fascination. I would stare out of the window at the sky for hours.'*

Raymond remembers being in two worlds at the same time:

> *'I saw a normal face and a face within a face. There were normal things and other things on top of them, a side real world within another world.'*

It is not surprising that people with schizophrenia should behave so strangely when their world has altered so dramatically. Many of their delusions stem directly from these perceptual changes. If they perceive strangers in the street to be making faces at them and if even buildings seem to be making threatening gestures, it is no wonder that they come to believe the world is against them.

Painting a Schizophrenic World

Because of the radically altered views of reality experienced by people with schizophrenia, their paintings and drawings are often revealingly bizarre. (It is worth noting that schizophrenia, at least in its early stages, does not hinder and may indeed enhance a person's creative potential. Not only is Vincent Van Gogh thought to have been schizophrenic, but so was Richard Dadd, the nineteenth-century English artist who painted delicate rural scenes peopled with fairies, pale women and effete men. Dadd killed his father as a consequence of his schizophrenic delusions. Louis Wain, famous for his pictures of cats, also suffered from schizophrenia.

Three of the themes of schizophrenic art are a preoccupation with detail at the expense of background, a morbid fascination with space, and an interest in classification for classification's sake. It is as if the painter can no longer perceive a coherent, organized world, as if orientation has disappeared, and as if it is impossible to distinguish what is important and what is not. The preoccupation with detail and fascination with classifying shapes, as if to bring order to chaos, can be seen in the case of a man aged 22 at the Bethlem Hospital, Kent, in the 1930s. This man was fascinated with chimneys. He gave each of them a name which was in fact a neologism. There were 'square ham' chimneys, 'callers', 'calculetters', 'prontches' and 'homos'. His explanations for these names were also bizarre:

Calculetter: letter comes from the noise of a steam engine that has that kind of chimney. Calcu is the same kind of word as caller.

Prontch: that word came when I was young. I can't tell its meaning.

Homo: this is a Latin word, it gave a Roman picture. There is a chimney like that in Catford which I saw against a hill and that hill reminded me of Rome.

One patient, Sarah, was also fascinated by what might be considered the non-essential features of a house – chimneys, garden gates, dustbins. Her eye seemed to be drawn to these details rather than the main structure. Clare, another patient under my care, presented her paintings at various stages of her life. The first was a relatively accomplished painting that she did when she was a normal art student. At the height of her schizophrenic illness, she produced two paintings, one of herself and one of a horse, both of which demonstrated a total change in her perception. When she recovered she made a living from painting very delicate miniatures for an Indian guru, not an abnormal thing to do in itself, but indicative of her interest in detail.

EXPERIENCING TIME AND SPACE
A schizophrenic's notion of both time and of space is affected by his or her disorders of thinking and perception. We are accustomed to a world in which things happen in a known sequence and in which things exist side by side or in the foreground or background. It is hard for us to imagine how time and space could be anything other than they are. Unless we are professional philosophers, we rarely give them much thought. Time may appear to drag if we are bored or speed past if we are enjoying ourselves, but that is about as much as we can

understand. For someone with schizophrenia, however, the whole fabric of existence changes. Time, and particularly space, are profoundly affected. Even more than their altered experience of things, it is hard for them to convey to us what this is like. Martin:

> 'Time seemed to be infinity. I thought I was controlling time. I thought I was here and in a different dimension at the same time.'

John:

> 'It seemed like I was back in the past, not today's time.'

Stephen came to distrust all the usual measures of time. He thought that all the newspapers published in London contained the incorrect date and so he travelled to the first town north of London which had its own local paper to find the correct date. He remembered as a child visiting a famous beauty spot to the south of London where his father had pointed out a fallen tree and explained how you could tell its age by the number of rings on the trunks. He felt that if only he could revisit the spot he would have a true measure of time.

Some of the accounts given earlier in this chapter, particularly Desmond's, contain references to disorientation in space. Surroundings that are normally familiar, for example, suddenly look strange. This is a common experience in the early stage of schizophrenia. It sometimes causes an intense fear of going out, similar to the agoraphobia which occurs in anxiety states. James:

> 'I was on a bridge in Chatham and I could go no further, a sense of vertigo.'

More commonly the person with schizophrenia feels lost, unable to recognize landmarks. Martin:

'There was a time when I went for a walk and I didn't know where I was.'

Rupert became preoccupied with the spatial aspects of things. He spent all his time at home cutting out cardboard shapes of all sizes and dimensions, claiming that he was inventing a new form of geometry.

Eugene Minkowski, a French psychiatrist between the two World Wars, considered that a 'morbid preoccupation with geometry' was one of the essential features of schizophrenic thinking. One of his patients described an obsession with 'the solidity of things':

> I was tormented [he wrote in his autobiography] by the vaults in churches. I could not accept that all that weight could be supported by ribs, pillars and a keystone. I could not understand why it did not fall down. I could not see why the cement in the free stones did not crumble because it must be a particularly vulnerable pressure point. I concluded that houses stayed up only through some terrestrial attraction. I came to doubt my own senses.

EMOTIONAL RESPONSES

Most people with schizophrenia have emotional responses which are appropriate to what is going on in their lives. So, if they see people around them pulling hideous faces or believe that they are Jesus Christ, their mood will reflect this – fright in the former case, perhaps, and elation in the latter. Their range of emotions is no different from anyone else's. Many of us suffer at times from some degree of depression – mild, moderate or severe – and this is just the same for people who suffer from schizophrenia. It is a surprising fact that at any given time about 1 in 10 of otherwise normal people will be going through at least a moderate depressive phase. This is also true of people with schizophrenia. The 19-century American writer Henry Thoreau referred to the human condition rather pessimistically in the following way: 'Each of us lives a life of quiet desperation.' This is no less or more true of those with schizophrenia.

Heightened Emotions

Although no single emotion is lacking in schizophrenics and all occur at more or less the same rate, there *is* a way in which the emotional life of people with schizophrenia is different from normal, and that is in the intensity with which any emotion is experienced. In the early stage of the illness there is often a heightening of all emotions. Andrew McGhie and James Chapman, two Scottish psychologists working in the 1950s, placed great emphasis on this intensification of experience at the outset of schizophrenia. They considered that normal people filter sensations from the outside world according to their inclination and current task in hand. Schizophrenia, they believed, was caused by a breakdown in this filter, which then led the person to be flooded and overwhelmed by anything and everything that was going on around them. It was an attractive theory at the time, and although this is now discredited the two psychologists were at least aware of the value of simply listening to what people with schizophrenia say about their experiences. One of their patients said this about the intensification of emotions:

> You have no idea what it's like, doctor. You would have to experience it yourself. When you feel yourself going into a sort of coma you get really scared. It's like waiting on a landing craft going into D-Day. You tremble and panic. It's like no other fear on earth.

Karl Jaspers, a German psychiatrist at the turn of the century (considered by many to be the most brilliant psychiatrist this century), believed schizophrenia in its early stages brought out a person's creative spirit. He singled out Van Gogh the painter and Hölderlin the poet as those whose creativity was enhanced by schizophrenia:

> Why is schizophrenia in its initial stages so often a process of cosmic, religious or metaphysical revelation? It is an extremely impressive fact: this exhibition of fine and subtle understanding, this impossible shattering piano performance, this masterly creativity.
>
> (JASPERS, 1913)

Blunted Emotions

As schizophrenia progresses, however, particularly in the days before effective treatment was available, the opposite of emotional intensification occurs. People with schizophrenia then complain that they feel no emotion or less emotion than before.

Sean:

> At the beginning of my illness I was suffering inwardly ... a sense of despair almost amounting to terror came on. Later this was replaced by flattening. I would respond to people very flatly. I became the opposite of spontaneous – diffident, more laboured.

James:

> I just don't seem to get any pleasure out of anything. I look at other people as they go about their lives and think, 'Why can't I be like them?' I seem to be empty inside. Nothing touches

me anymore. It is as if I'm an object without feelings, without
the urge to do anything.

Psychiatrists call this inability to feel pleasure *Anhedonia*.
(*Hedonic*, from the Greek, means 'pleasure-seeking', and
anhedonic is the opposite of this.) Schizophrenics who complain of this usually betray less emotion in their facial expression, tone of voice and gesture than normal people, and these
outward signs are termed *flattening* or *blunting of affect* by psychiatrists. (The terms mood, affect and emotion can be used
interchangeably.) Schizophrenics with anhedonia usually complain bitterly of it. It is one of the most distressing features of
the condition and is the one thing that most commonly drives
them to suicide. This is quite understandable, as life without
joy or without even the prospect of joy must be unbearable.
One patient put his hand into a fire and was badly burnt.
When asked why he did this, he replied that he wanted to feel
some emotion, any emotion, rather than continue in the dull
world in which he found himself.

The Wrong Emotion
Some people with schizophrenia show emotions which appear
to be out of keeping with the situation at the time. They may
giggle when the situation calls for a serious mood, or be seen
laughing to themselves. Psychiatrists call this *inappropriate
affect*. One patient tried to explain why it happens:

> It must look queer to people when I laugh about something
> that has got nothing to do with what I am talking about, but
> they don't know what's going on inside and how much of it is
> running round in my head.

ACTION AND INACTION

As we have seen, people with schizophrenia enter a new world that bears no relation to reality and in which everything – their ways of thinking and of perceiving everything around them – is altered. Even the experience of movement may be altered. For most of us, routine actions such as walking or running rarely impinge on our consciousness. We don't have to think about doing them, we just do them automatically. Even a more complex action, such as driving a car, is almost automatic for the experienced driver. It is only if some hazard presents itself that we pay full attention to the task. This is not to say that we are bad drivers; on the contrary, the task is so well learned that we can relegate it to our subconscious and as we drive home, release space in our consciousness for more interesting matters, wondering what we shall have for dinner, for example, or thinking about the day's events.

Life is more complicated for people with schizophrenia. Some find that they cannot free their conscious minds of routine tasks in this way. They are acutely aware of every step of an action. Some patients are almost brought to a standstill because of this:

> I am not sure of my own movements any more. It's very hard to describe this but at times I am not sure about even simple actions like sitting down. It's not so much thinking out what to do, it's the doing of it that sticks me. [Other] people just do things, but I have to watch first to see how [to] do things. I have to do everything step by step. Nothing is automatic now. Everything has to be considered.

Psychiatrists consider a disorder of posture and movement to be an uncommon but integral part of schizophrenia. It is known as *catatonia*. The patient quoted above is describing one aspect of this.

A DISTORTED REALITY

The psychosis of schizophrenia transports the sufferer from a relatively ordered, organized existence to a world in which nothing is familiar and some elements of life may be nightmarish and distressing. This chapter has shown how every aspect of a schizophrenic's existence – thoughts and perceptions, sensations, emotions, a feeling for time and space and even co-ordination of the body – can no longer be relied upon. The next chapter explores this distorted reality, and distinguishes schizophrenia from other forms of mental illness.

2

WHAT IS SCHIZOPHRENIA?

The diagnosis of schizophrenia is currently made through a combined process of establishing what schizophrenia *is* and what it is *not*. Schizophrenia is only one form of psychiatric disorder (*see Figure, pages 26–27*). All psychiatrists and most other professionals therefore have to rely for a diagnosis on systematically eliminating all the other possible types of psychiatric disorders.

In order to understand the true nature of schizophrenia, it is essential to appreciate a further point. This is the distinction between *psychiatric disorder* and *mental illness*. They are not the same thing. The term psychiatric disorder is much wider than what is meant by mental illness. A habitual offender may be referred by the courts for a psychiatric opinion before sentencing. The psychiatrist may find that the person has had a deprived childhood, has now developed into an aggressive and unhappy adult and may be a drug addict and a heavy drinker as well. He (for it is usually a man) does have a psychiatric disorder in the sense that his behaviour is causing distress to himself and to others, but he is not mentally ill.

Mental illness, on the other hand, is a *subgroup* of psychiatric disorder, in which (1) there are distinct and recognizable psychological changes; (2) there has been an obvious change in the person from his or her previous mental state to the present one; and (3) the person cannot really help how he or she is now – the mind is altered from within.

This distinction between psychiatric disorders in general and mental illness is not an easy one to grasp at first, and has been disputed by some professionals in related fields (though more so in the 1960s than now). It is a real distinction, however, and appreciating it is the first step in understanding schizophrenia itself. Schizophrenia is both a psychiatric disorder and mental illness.

The next step is to appreciate that schizophrenia is not the *only* mental illness. For the purposes of simplicity we can say that there are 11 mental illnesses in all, of which schizophrenia is one. They are defined on pages 26–27 and discussed in detail in this chapter.

As well as explaining how psychiatrists diagnose schizophrenia, understanding the other types of psychiatric disorders and mental illnesses also helps to clarify some of the myths and misconceptions surrounding schizophrenia. Understanding the true nature of the illness is important both for the sufferers themselves and, as seen from Chapter 1, for the sufferers' family and friends.

The Correct Diagnosis

Developing a 'feel' for what schizophrenia is and for what it is not is essential in making a correct diagnosis at the outset – in other words, at the onset of the illness. Not only is it important that the diagnosis is correct (as this affects treatment and recovery) but also that it is made, ideally, within a short time of the person becoming ill.

Many people with schizophrenia will have been entirely

normal until their first breakdown, and many will return to normal reality if they are promptly treated. Only one in four may have been a little 'odd' before their breakdown (and this is described more fully in Chapter 4, under the heading What About the Adult Personality?)

As you will see in this chapter and in Chapter 3, the diagnosis of schizophrenia is fraught with difficulties and complexities, partly born of the similarities it bears, in some respects, to other forms of psychiatric disorder.

DOUBTS ABOUT DIAGNOSIS

Doctors, as well as lay-people, make mistakes in diagnosing schizophrenia. One common one, for example, is to diagnose mania instead of schizophrenia, or schizophrenia instead of mania. Either way this is serious because the correct treatment for each condition is entirely different. If the schizophrenia remains untreated, or is incorrectly treated, it may persist. This sort of mistake can be made by general practitioners, junior psychiatrists and quite often by consultant psychiatrists, which is why it is worth taking responsibility for the initial diagnosis and taking very seriously the care and treatment of a sufferer – and, if necessary, discussing the matter with the patient's hospital consultant. Because of such complexities, a GP should always refer the patient to a consultant psychiatrist rather than making her or his own diagnosis. (Diagnosis is described more fully in Chapter 3.)

Psychiatric Classification

The full range of psychiatric disorders is set out below. Only those defined in Levels 1 and 2 are mental illnesses. Those defined in Levels 3 and 4 are not.

Classification of Psychiatric Disorders and the 11 Types of Mental Illness

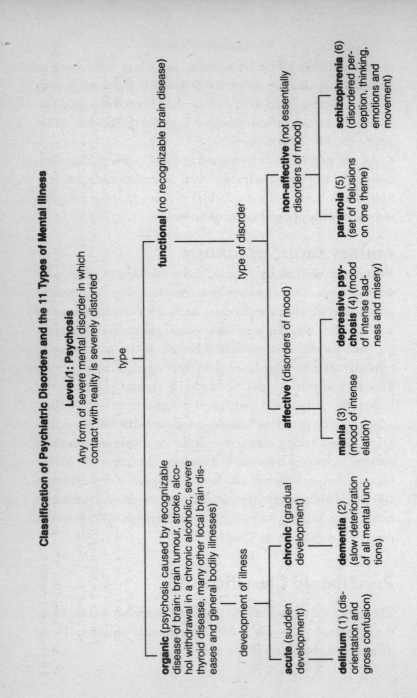

Level 1: Psychosis
Any form of severe mental disorder in which contact with reality is severely distorted

type

organic (psychosis caused by recognizable disease of brain: brain tumour, stroke, alcohol withdrawal in a chronic alcoholic, severe thyroid disease, many other local brain diseases and general bodily illnesses)

development of illness

acute (sudden development)

delirium (1) (disorientation and gross confusion)

chronic (gradual development)

dementia (2) (slow deterioration of all mental functions)

functional (no recognizable brain disease)

type of disorder

affective (disorders of mood)

mania (3) (mood of intense elation)

depressive psychosis (4) (mood of intense sadness and misery)

non-affective (not essentially disorders of mood)

paranoia (5) (set of delusions on one theme)

schizophrenia (6) (disordered perception, thinking, emotions and movement)

Level 2: Neurosis

Mental illness in which a person's sense of reality remains intact

types

depressive (7) (extreme form of misery but going beyond what would be regarded as normal for the circumstances)

anxiety (8) (extreme form of anxious response but without any obvious trigger)

obsessional (9) (compulsions, including, for example, cleaning, checking, repeating, avoiding)

phobic (10) (phobias, including, for example, agoraphobia and phobias for heights, cats and spiders)

hysterical (11) (showing physical symptoms such as blindness, loss of sensation or paralysis for which there is no physical cause)

Level 3: Personality Disorder

This is a psychiatric classification of personality but not of mental illness. Someone who stands out from the average person by virtue of one or two character traits (for example, extremely shy [sensitive]; extremely prickly or touchy [paranoid]; extremely antisocial [psychopath]; and extremely eccentric [schizoid]).

Level 4: Normal Reaction

A normal person can go through a short period of distress after divorce or bereavement, for example. This distress may take the form of depression or anxiety but it is not a mental illness because it is so clearly caused by something that we can all understand. This type of reaction will clear in time or clear if the trigger is removed or resolved. Depressive illness or anxiety neurosis (see 7 and 8 above) will not clear even if the trigger is removed, because by this time there will have been a change in the brain chemicals; the condition then has to run its course or be treated medically.

You can see from this table that there are four main psychiatric classifications, only two of which (psychosis and neurosis) indicate the existence of mental illness. There are eleven types of mental illness (numbered in the table), of which schizophrenia is one.

PSYCHOSIS

Psychosis is the psychiatrists' term for madness. A psychotic person's *perceptions and thoughts about the world are no longer within our range of experience*. Their 'reality' is no longer our 'reality' and, try as we might, at some point we cannot reach them. They themselves usually have no insight into this change in reality, and regard their world as the real one. In practice we regard them as *deluded* – having false beliefs; *hallucinated* – having perceptions without any stimulus; or *thought disordered* – speaking or writing in a grossly abnormal way.

NEUROSIS

A neurosis, on the other hand, is a mental illness which does not alter a person's sense of reality. There are no hallucinations, no delusions and no gross thought disorder. Its basis is usually an abnormal mood – anxiety, depression, fear – which causes the person to behave and think differently compared with before. A neurosis is almost always self-limiting and a disturbed period in someone's life. In other words, you cannot have a life-long neurosis. A person is normal until the neurosis starts (usually while in his or her twenties or thirties). The neurosis lasts a certain length of time – usually six months to two years if untreated – and then clears up, leaving the person the same as before. In everyday language the term 'neurotic' is sometimes used to describe a personality type (Level 3 in my scheme): 'He's a very neurotic person,' meaning that he has always been anxious, fearful or moody. Psychiatrists, however, restrict the use of the term to all non-psychotic illnesses – Level 2 in my scheme. A neurosis is not always less severe than a psychosis. One can have a mild schizophrenia or a severe obsessional neurosis. For this reason some neuroses can be confused with schizophrenia.

PERSONALITY DISORDER

To say that someone has a personality disorder means that you consider that he has always been unusual or different in some respect from the average person. Someone with a personality disorder is not ill. His personality has always been the same; it is a life-long condition, or at least since the adult personality was taking shape in late adolescence. Any prominent psychological characteristic that sets the person apart from the rest of us is known as a *personality trait*, and this then gives its name to the personality disorder. For example, if someone is particularly moody or sensitive or prickly one can say that he has a personality disorder characterized by moodiness, sensitivity or prickliness. The habitual offender mentioned at the start of this chapter might be regarded as having an explosive personality disorder.

Psychiatrists are sometimes criticized for labelling people too readily, but to say that someone has a particular personality disorder means only that you have identified an important aspect of that person. It allows you to predict how he will react in certain situations. Someone with a personality disorder may come to psychiatric attention because his life is in a mess and someone has thought he was ill. Usually it turns out that there is a mismatch between his personality and his current life situation. If he had a different personality he would be ideally suited to his life situation, or if he changed his life circumstances he would equally well be content. It is what I call the 'round peg in the square hole syndrome'. Psychiatrists are no better than any other counsellor, professional or lay, in pointing this out. Sometimes sufferers do appear on superficial acquaintance to be mentally ill. When I worked in a general hospital, I was occasionally called to the medical ward because a physically ill patient had, it was alleged by the nurses, 'gone mad', refusing treatment or threatening to discharge himself and being generally uncooperative. On careful enquiry it would turn out that the patient had no sign at all of any mental illness but instead had a life-long resentment of authority in any form. The uncooperative attitude was predictable when one knew how the person had fared at school, work and in other situations where rules had had to be obeyed. Such people might be regarded as having a paranoid personality disorder.

We shall see later on that the distinction between some types of personality disorders and schizophrenia is not always easy. It is made more difficult by the fact that someone with a personality disorder is just as likely (if not more likely) as a normal person to develop a true mental illness.

NORMAL REACTION

The fourth Level one might think has nothing to do with psychiatry at all. Surely a normal person doesn't need to see a psychiatrist and certainly shouldn't be confused with a schizophrenic or even as someone with one of the neuroses. If this were so, the practice of psychiatry would be easy. As we all know, however, what is regarded as normal behaviour varies enormously from generation to generation, from place to place and from culture to culture. Dyeing your hair green and piercing your nose with a safety pin would be regarded as extremely abnormal if you were a middle-aged vicar's wife in a small country town in the 1930s, but not if you were a punk teenager in London in the early 1980s. This is why it is so difficult to practise psychiatry within another culture, with its own beliefs about religion, health and other important matters. Even within one's own culture there are huge differences in how people respond to stress and what stressors they react to. An incident which one person might shrug off may have a devastating effect on another. This means that what is one person's normal reaction to an event can sometimes be mistaken for a true mental illness.

There are certain normal experiences, too, that are sometimes taken as symptoms of a mental illness, because people or their relatives are not aware that they are normal. A good example is the experience of hearing footsteps on the stairs or seeing a silhouette of a figure just as you are about to fall asleep. Several times I have been referred patients with no more than this because their general practitioner thought they were schizophrenic. These experiences are entirely normal and are known as hypnagogic hallucinations (from the Greek *hypnos*, for 'sleep').

Varieties of Psychosis

Psychoses are conventionally divided into two types: organic and functional. An organic psychosis is one in which the direct cause is a recognizable disease of the brain. A brain tumour, stroke, alcohol withdrawal in a chronic alcoholic, severe thyroid disease, and many other local brain diseases and generalized bodily illnesses can cause an organic psychosis. A functional psychosis is one in which recognizable brain disease is not present; it can be identified only by ensuring that definite brain damage is not there, by, for instance, carrying out a scan of the brain.

The division into organic and functional psychoses is only provisional, however, reflecting the state of knowledge at the current time. Many psychiatrists, including myself, believe that schizophrenia is caused by brain disease and should therefore be classified as organic, but there are at the moment no definitive tests to prove that this is so. In the mean time, therefore, schizophrenia has to be regarded as a functional psychosis.

DELIRIUM

The form that a true organic psychosis takes depends on whether the physical cause has begun acutely – over a matter of hours or days, producing a dramatic change in behaviour; or has progressed slowly – over weeks, months or years. If it begins quite suddenly it is known as delirium; if it represents a slow deterioration of mental functions, such as memory and concentration, it is dementia.

A good example of an acute organic psychosis is that seen in a chronic alcoholic who decides to stop drinking, and here there may be the visual hallucinations, delusions of persecution and gross confusion that are all typical of an acute organic psychosis. For the first 24 hours, he (because it is usually a man) feels a little shaky and unwell, and then quite suddenly during the next 24 hours becomes acutely psychotic – quite mad. He starts seeing things which are not there. These visual hallucinations are usually of animals or people and are exactly as in real life, except that they are often brightly coloured and on the move all the time. A patient of mine saw chicken livers dripping blood falling down the stairs. This hallucination illustrates the general rule, although they were animal only in origin. Stories about alcoholics seeing pink rats, green men or elephants are quite correct – they do. There may also be delusions of persecution: gangs of men trying to murder them is a common theme. The most characteristic feature of an acute organic psychosis, however, is a gross confusion. They do not know the date or even the year, have no idea where they are and don't recognize people around them. Their thinking is very muddled and their mood is usually one of terror.

The effect of illegal drugs may also be mistaken for schizophrenia because certain drugs, such as amphetamines (speed), can induce hallucinations and delusions. Mistaking drug-induced organic psychoses for schizophrenia, and vice versa, is more common than failing to distinguish alcoholic psychoses from schizophrenia. This is because alcoholic psychoses tend to include more visual hallucinations and confusion than either schizophrenia or drug-induced states. Moreover, the peak onset of schizophrenia, particularly in men, is in the late teens and may therefore coincide with the period in which adolescents experiment with drugs such as amphetamines, LSD, and possibly cannabis, which may cause hallucinations; an alcoholic psychosis rarely occurs before the age of 40 because it needs 10 or even 20 years of heavy drinking to be produced. The point about drug-induced states involving illegal use of amphetamines and the like is that they are milder forms of delirium, where the person may not be all that confused but will still have a set of hallucinations and delusions which are substantially different from those occurring in someone with schizophrenia.

Distinguishing Delirium from Schizophrenia

Gross confusion, muddled thinking and a mood of terror are a group of symptoms known as delirium or 'toxic confusional state'. The condition is more or less the same no matter what the physical cause, provided that it is acute (starts quite suddenly).

Delirium is quite different from schizophrenia. The visual perceptual changes in schizophrenia, as shown in Chapter 1, tend to be illusions and distortions, particularly regarding the way in which things relate to each other. And when true visual hallucinations do occur in schizophrenia they are superimposed onto real things – a peculiar eye on a normal face is typical. Schizophrenics virtually never see things such as animals, which aren't there at all. Their delusions, too, are different. Schizophrenic delusions tend to have a predictable set of themes, mainly involving control by an outside agency. In acute organic psychosis, the themes are persecution and a feeling that something dreadful is happening to other people in the near vicinity. People with schizophrenia are egocentric, in this respect. Their delusions are centred on themselves and they rarely include events happening to other people.

Delirium should, in view of these points, rarely be mistaken for schizophrenia. Unfortunately it often is, particularly by junior doctors in medicine and surgery. To recap, its chief differences from schizophrenia are the recognizable physical cause, gross confusion, lifelike visual hallucinations and terrifying persecutory delusions involving other people.

DEMENTIA

Senile dementia is the chronic organic psychosis with which most people will be familiar. Here the entire brain degenerates. Sometimes there is a treatable cause, such as vitamin deficiency, but this is rare. Most often there is not, and the condition is most commonly due to Alzheimer's disease. Alzheimer's dementia is rare before the age of 60 but becomes more common with each decade thereafter, hence it is responsible for the large majority of cases of senile dementia. A chronic organic psychosis does bear a superficial resemblance to schizophrenia, particularly if the schizophrenia has been left untreated or is resistant to treatment.

There is an important historical link between dementia and schizophrenia; this is only a historical link but it is unfortunately misleading to some of today's psychiatrists, as we will see in the next section on distinguishing dementia from schizophrenia. The link is that Emil Kraepelin (the German psychiatrist who first recognized what is now called schizophrenia as a definite illness in 1896) called it not schizophrenia but dementia praecox – praecox meaning early onset. He thought schizophrenia was a form of senile dementia occurring in late adolescence rather than in old age. He was, as it turned out, wrong about this, and Eugen Bleuler soon changed the name to schizophrenia because of this. Bleuler commented:

> In schizophrenia, even when well-advanced, all the simple mental functions, as far as we know, are intact. In particular memory, unlike the case in true dementia, is unaffected. One may find surprisingly that under an apparent envelope of dementia the intelligence is much less affected than one might imagine, as if it were only asleep.

Eugen Bleuler's metaphor 'as if it were only asleep' is very apt. In the days before effective treatment people with schizophrenia had to remain in hospital for most of their lives, and in particularly severe cases they would sit motionless for much of the time.

Other psychiatrists have referred to schizophrenia as an orchestra without a conductor and as an engine without fuel. True dementia is the exact opposite of this. Individual mental functions gradually deteriorate but the person manages to keep up a social front for many years. They are able to appear intellectually abler than they are and to cover up their deficiencies. People with schizophrenia, on the other hand, appear worse than they actually are, as if they don't know how to use even the normal or superior intelligence that is theirs.

Albert is a good example of someone with moderate dementia. He was a man of 68 referred to me by his solicitor, who was concerned about Albert's ability to manage his affairs. Up until five years previously he had been the energetic and successful financial director of a big engineering company. Following a takeover, some financial irregularities were discovered and, after years of legal wrangling, he was eventually charged with fraud. His solicitor believed that he was now unfit to stand trial because he could not remember with sufficient clarity the business transactions which were the focus of the charges.

I visited him at home. His wife asked if she could stay in the room while I interviewed him. He offered me a drink and answered briefly but correctly my questions about his background. In fact his wife knew more about his background than he did. For the first half hour of the interview I could detect nothing seriously wrong with him. He laughed about his occasional lapses of memory, saying that his wife had always teased him about this. Then he said something which gave the game away. I asked about his son, whom I knew to be 28, because I had interviewed him the day before. Albert said: 'Well, he's a good boy. He's just left school. Going to Oxford University, you know.' He was 10 years out of date. When I pointed this out to him he began crying. His mental disability had been discovered and he was embarrassed at my observing his true mental state. In fact I had learned from his son the day before that Albert had all the features of a typical true dementia.

Albert looked older than his 68 years and his eyes were dull, as if there was no sparkle left in him. His mood when I saw him was flat and apathetic, but it is quite characteristic to hear a relative of someone with dementia say that he or she can be over-emotional and irritable at other times. Albert would only talk when spoken to; he would never initiate any conversation himself. When he did answer he said as little as possible and what he said was rather empty of content – small talk, cocktail party superficialities. At times he repeated himself. He had had no abnormal perceptual experiences, and these are indeed unusual in dementia. Albert had said to his wife, however, that he thought his son was stealing his money. This is quite a characteristic delusion in dementia – that a near relative or neighbour is trying to take one's possessions. His memory, particularly for recent events, was very patchy. I would have expected him, as a financial director, to have known about other financial scandals which were in the news at the time, but he did not. However, none of this was apparent at the beginning of the interview. In his own flat, with his wife to help him cover up, Albert could maintain a social poise and appearance of normality for a good half hour.

Distinguishing Dementia from Schizophrenia

I have dealt with the symptoms of true dementia at length because some modern-day psychiatrists are trying to prove that Emil Kraepelin was correct to link schizophrenia with dementia. I believe that this is misguided. Knowledge about how the brain functions has progressed considerably since the 19th century, and one can now say with reasonable confidence that schizophrenia *is* a brain disease, but one where a *particular* part of the brain fails to function, and not simply a *global* and overall dementia.

To recap on the chief differences between dementia and schizophrenia: the former is a progressive deterioration of the entire brain which causes memory loss and apathy, alternating with over-emotionality and irritability, and an impoverishment of thinking with fleeting delusions about theft and harassment by those around. Social poise can be maintained until the terminal stages of the illness. In dementia, unlike schizophrenia, a definite physical abnormality of the brain can be uncovered. In Albert's case, for example, a brain scan showed marked shrinkage of the brain substance.

MANIA

The next psychosis to be distinguished from schizophrenia is mania. This is called an *affective psychosis* or manic-depressive psychosis because, like a severe depression (to be considered next), the central feature is an abnormal 'affect' or mood. In mania the abnormal mood is elation and all the abnormal perceptions and thoughts stem from this. If a manic person has hallucinations they will be consistent with this mood. The person may hear a voice saying, 'You should be King, only you can do the job' or 'You are God's chosen person, you must carry out his commands.' Delusions are also grandiose. Sufferers may believe that they can do miraculous things, that they are on a special mission to save the world or that they are Christ himself. Their thoughts are speeded up and this shows itself in what psychiatrists call *pressure of speech* and *flight of ideas*. They are so full of ideas that they cannot stop talking about them, and each idea immediately suggests another, giving the impression that they are jumping from one half-baked thought to another.

Gary had a typical manic illness. At the age of 18 he developed appendicitis. His appendix was removed in what appeared to be a routine operation, but five days later he started behaving totally out of character. He began calling his parents by their first names, something he had never done before. Before the operation he was rather tight with his money, but now he asked his parents for a loan to buy an aquarium fully stocked with as many tropical fish as possible. Rather a quiet boy, Gary now kept his parents up till 2 in the morning telling them about his plans for the future. In fact he seemed to need no sleep at all. He stayed up the rest of the night scribbling his ideas down or listening to music. He had always been interested in football, but now thought that he was being offered a trial for his local professional club. He also thought that he was an accredited film critic for his local newspaper. Gary had left school with only moderate grades in domestic science and rural science. He now maintained, however, that he had passed all his school-leaving exams with flying colours, including an exam in 'nuclear physiology'. He was not disorientated in time — he knew what the day of the week was and the year — but occasionally believed he was the Messiah, and that he was surrounded by Biblical characters such as David and Goliath.

Gary's parents believed that the hospital was to blame for his illness. However, his mother had also suffered a breakdown, in her case a depressive illness after a hysterectomy, and I felt that there was a genetic predisposition (a family tendency) to manic-depressive psychosis. The operation was thus a trigger for the illness rather than the direct cause.

Distinguishing Mania from Schizophrenia

Mania, or hypomania (which is the same thing), is often mistaken for schizophrenia. It is probably the most common mistake made by psychiatrists, and in both directions – mania when the true diagnosis is schizophrenia, and schizophrenia when it is really mania. It is a serious mistake because the correct treatment for each condition is entirely different. Mania almost always responds to the drug lithium, a salt which stabilizes mood. It halts a manic episode which is in progress and prevents further episodes. If antischizophrenic drugs are given this will tranquillize the person but will not cure him. On the other hand, lithium has no effect at all in schizophrenia, which means that the schizophrenia will persist.

At the height of a manic episode, sufferers are so psychotic, so mad, that the crucial link between their delusions or hallucinations and their mood is not always clear-cut. In fact, the mood of a manic person is sometimes one of irritability rather than elation. And, when very psychotic, they may be flitting so fast from idea to idea that they appear to be formally thought disordered (*see Chapter 1*): their speech or writings are gibberish. They may even have some of the delusions which are typical of schizophrenia (*see Chapter 1*), with a theme of control by outside influences.

Only a careful assessment of the entire illness, with particular regard to how it started and its early symptoms, can help in this distinction. In my experience, many psychiatrists often ignore a relative's crucial information regarding *how a mental illness has begun*, preferring to rely on their own impressions of how a sufferer is *at the time* that they see him or her. In distinguishing between mania and schizophrenia, this is a serious error.

Mania is characterized by persistent elated or irritable mood, hallucinations and delusions which are grandiose or religiose in content, pressure of speech and flight of ideas. Although some people with schizophrenia are at times elated or irritable, and may sometimes talk quickly with disconnected ideas, such phases do not last, whereas in a manic illness they persist throughout. Manic people have an infectious gaiety about them. They make you laugh; they want to involve you in their schemes and are what is called *disinhibited* – they overstep social boundaries, for example, by calling doctors by their first names, kissing strangers and intruding into your personal life. They behave like extreme extroverts, always seeking new adventures and new stimulation.

People with schizophrenia usually behave in the opposite fashion: they fail to engage you in their lives, and if they try to enter the world of someone else it is in a naïve and gauche way. There is no infectious quality to their occasional elated phases and no righteous indignation or attempted justification behind their irritability. Their emotions, like their perceptions and ideas, are beyond our ken. Mania, however, is not difficult to understand as a gross exaggeration of normal high spirits.

DEPRESSION

Depression is a universal human response. Very few of us can say that we do not know what it is like. Depression is also the name for a mental illness – depressive illness – which can be neurotic (Level 2) or psychotic (Level 1) in type.

The use of the same word to cover very different states of mind is confusing for all of us, psychiatrists included. At the beginning of this century, depressive illness was called melancholia to separate it from the state of 'normal misery' – misery being a normal human response to an unfortunate event – brought on by a bereavement or a disappointment over unfulfilled expectations. In the figure on pages 26–27 this sort of depression would appear at Level 4 as a normal reaction.

A depressed or morbid outlook on life can also be a personality trait. People with a pronounced attitude to life of this nature can be thought of as having a depressive personality disorder (Level 3). They always look on the black side. They are not ill; they just seem to have been born two drinks behind, as it were. Psychiatrists call such people *dysthymic* personalities – from the Greek *thymus* for 'mood' and *dys* meaning 'disordered'. Sometimes they swing back and forth between mild elation one day and misery the next for no apparent reason. This is known as a *cyclothymic* personality disorder. These people are sometimes called manic depressive, but this is not the label that a psychiatrist would attach, as they are not actually ill.

Depression is also the name given to a mental illness, in fact two mental illnesses if one regards neurotic and psychotic depression as separate, which is what I have done in the list on pages 26–27. Some psychiatrists dispute the fact that they are separate, but for our purposes this does not matter. It is the psychotic variety, whether a separate illness or not, which can be confused with schizophrenia.

The essential features of a depressive psychosis, as with mania, is a profound change of mood. Everything else stems from this. Sufferers look depressed, feel depressed and this colours their entire outlook on life – past, present and future.

They maintain that they have let everyone down in the past and failed miserably in all they have attempted. They may exaggerate some mild misdemeanour in their past life into a major crime. One of my patients, a man now in his eighties, had contracted venereal disease while on leave from the army during the First World War. This was before he met his wife, but he now believed the event had cast a blight on both their entire lives.

Sufferers feel incapable of doing anything, everything is an effort, their concentration is poor and they lose interest in their usual activities. They sleep badly, typically waking early, and have no appetite. Their mood may improve as the day wears on but they dread going to sleep because they know how dreadful they will feel the next morning. The future looks particularly bleak, and suicidal thoughts are never far from their mind.

In the psychotic form of depression there are delusions of worthlessness, guilt and bodily decay. Patients believe they have ruined other people's lives by their previous actions and that they should be punished for this. Their body feels diseased with cancer, for example, and in extreme cases they may even deny that parts of it work at all or even exist: they claim to have no insides or that their bowels are blocked. If they hear voices these are invariably derogatory: 'You're no good, you deserve to die.'

Louise had a typical depressive psychosis. She had been well all her life until the age of 66. She was happily married and her husband had just retired. She had brought up two children, one of whom had just taken up a job in Newcastle. This event had a profound effect on her. She became agitated and announced to her husband that she had to go to Newcastle to atone for her past sins. He asked her what she meant and she told him for the first time that she had had an illegitimate child before she knew him and that he had been adopted by a couple in Newcastle. Her husband was quite understanding about the matter, but she believed that it had ruined their lives. For the next three years she was in and out of hospital with severe agitation and inability to cope. When at home she would spend all her time constantly vacuuming all the rooms because she thought they were dirty. A home visit by one of my staff revealed that they were spotless. She also said that she had no clothes to wear although her wardrobe was quite adequate. She looked as if she had all the cares in the world on her shoulders and she refused to believe she would ever get better. I began to think so myself, because none of the usual treatments for depression had the slightest effect on her. Then one weekend she suddenly improved and has remained well for the past two years.

Unlike schizophrenia, there is usually an event which triggers off a depressive illness, but what makes it a depressive illness rather than just normal distress is the *quality* of the symptoms. Louise's belief that everything around her was dirty, which was quite untrue, shows that the depression had spread, as it were, to colour areas of her life that had nothing to do with the original event.

Distinguishing Depression from Schizophrenia
Schizophrenia is most likely to be confused with a depressive psychosis only when the schizophrenia is at its earliest stage. At that time, before hallucinations and delusions have crystallized, sufferers, experiencing the sort of perceptual changes and altered thinking I illustrated in Chapter 1, may respond by retiring to bed or closing in on themselves. To an observer they may appear depressed, and as they are often reluctant to describe what is happening their silence confirms this view in the observer.

Schizophrenia and depression are otherwise fairly easy to

distinguish, with the proviso that schizophrenics are just as likely to suffer all types of depression – psychosis, neurosis and normal reaction – as anyone else, as well as their schizophrenia. They can also have had cyclothymic personalities (been miserable or grumpy people) prior to their illness; this is less common, however, because the personality of a schizophrenic before the illness is either normal or restricted to one or two distinct personality types (and this will be discussed more fully in Chapter 4).

The fundamental difference between a severe depressive illness and schizophrenia is the prevailing *mood*. The main features in severe depression are what are known as *mood-congruent* – consistent with this mood – whereas in schizophrenia they are *mood-incongruent* – nothing to do with the prevailing mood. For example, if my patient Louise had said, when depressed, that she was going to Newcastle to escape from rays entering her head, this would be a mood-incongruent delusion, and I would not have diagnosed her as having a depressive psychosis. There are other differences, but these are less reliable – the age of the patient when the illness starts being the main one. A good rule of thumb is, if a mental illness begins for the first time between the ages of 40 and 60 it is likely to be depression and not schizophrenia. The risk of becoming depressed is constant at all age groups, whereas the risk of developing schizophrenia diminishes rapidly after the age of 40.

PARANOIA

Like many psychiatric words, the term paranoid has entered everyday language with a different meaning from that employed by psychiatrists. Its lay meaning is a prickly person, someone who is inclined to take everything personally and to be generally suspicious. The term is derived from the Greek word for madness, and until schizophrenia was identified at the turn of this century paranoia covered all types of madness which were neither definitely organic nor based on mood change. In our list (pages 26–27), therefore, non-affective psychosis would have had only one category in it – paranoia. When schizophrenia was identified, paranoia became a leftover term for all forms of psychosis which were neither organic, affective nor schizophrenic. This is how it is used today.

Two patients under my care illustrate what paranoia is. Christine was an intelligent 32-year-old who worked as an inspector of croupiers in a casino, making sure there was no collusion between croupiers and gamblers. She had been married briefly in her early twenties, but this had not worked out and she now lived alone in rented flats with hardly any social life at all. She originally consulted me because she was finding it difficult to remain in a flat for more than a month. After a week or so in a new flat she would experience an unpleasant smell – stale fish, sewage, sweaty clothes – it varied with each flat. She would then think that the smell had transferred to her own clothes, and that strangers on the bus or her colleagues at work were passing comments on it. She claimed to overhear them say, 'She smells strongly today' or 'Isn't it about time she washed her clothes?' In fact, Christine did dry-clean or wash her clothes every day and her hands were red and raw from continual washing. There were no other symptoms, although she subsequently took an overdose of tablets because she was so distressed by these experiences. In the three years that I knew her she moved flats no less than 46 times, losing a considerable amount of money in the process on lost deposits. In hospital the smell would disappear for the first week but then reappear and she would discharge herself claiming that the sewage supply was faulty.

She was not very co-operative with the treatment we offered her, either psychotherapy or drug treatment, as she refused to believe that the smells were imaginary or even exaggerations of normal. We even tested her sense of smell, in case she were unduly sensitive to smells, but she was a heavy smoker and if anything her sense of smell was less acute than other people's.

Christine's employers had no complaints about the quality of her work except for the fact that she was often late in starting work because she spent an hour in the shower washing all her clothes after the journey to work. She would not let us contact her relatives and was secretive about her past. She finally refused even to attend my outpatients' clinic because she felt that we had done nothing to help her.

Christine illustrates the essential feature of paranoia, which is that the psychosis is restricted to one theme only. From one false belief or one false perception everything else that follows is quite understandable and reasonable. Psychiatrists call this a *well-encapsulated psychosis*, because apart from the single hallucination or delusion the sufferer is mentally normal. It is as if the psychotic part of the person is within a capsule. Christine's pre-illness personality could be described as sensitive and prickly, but there were no features of depression or schizophrenia. Neither was there any brain disease. Damage to the part of the brain that is responsible for smell sometimes causes olfactory hallucinations, but investigations into this possibility proved negative.

The second patient, Ronald, has been under my care for 14 years. When I first met him he was a man of 37, who complained bitterly that he was being harassed in the street, in the newspaper and on the telephone by people continually referring to his having caused a girl's death. He first became aware of this when he saw a headline in a popular newspaper with the words 'Ronald, the woman hater'. The article had nothing to do with him in reality but he thought it did. This is known as a *delusion of reference*, referring something to yourself which is completely independent of you. It was from that moment that he developed the notion that he had murdered a woman.

He drew all sorts of other incidents, past and present, into his delusional system. He had once had a homosexual experience in the Navy and this was a further matter about which he claimed he was being harassed. If the phone rang but when picked up the caller put the receiver down, this was put down to harassment. If someone looked at him in a particular way, this too was a direct reference either to his sexual orientation or to his crime. These ideas have continued more or less unchanged for the whole time I have known him. Drug treatment is of little use and psychotherapy comes up against a brick wall because his beliefs are so strong. Despite this he has continued to work well as a bookbinder, pursue his hobbies and care for his elderly mother.

Ronald, like Christine, illustrates the single delusional theme (a set of delusions on a single theme) which is the hallmark of paranoia. Although Ronald later drew into his theme a variety of other incidents, they were all connected somehow to the original theme. As well as being called well-encapsulated, these psychoses are also called *well-systematized* because the logical system spreads outwards from the original false conclusion, with every incident interconnecting with another.

Other common themes seen in paranoia are extreme unwarranted jealousy, known as *morbid jealousy*; the idea that someone socially superior is in love with you despite their having given no indication of this, called *erotomania*; a relentless quest for legal reparation over some trivial incident in the past – *litigious paranoia*; an extreme preoccupation with bodily disease – *monosymptomatic hypochondriacal psychosis*; an extreme preoccupation with the shape of some parts of the body, particularly the nose – *dysmorphophobia* (from the Greek for 'fear of disordered shape').

It can be seen from these varieties that most paranoid themes are exaggerations of normal concerns. What makes the condition psychotic is the conviction with which the belief is held, against all evidence to the contrary, and the preoccupation with the matter to the detriment of other aspects of the person's life.

Distinguishing Paranoia from Schizophrenia

Most people with schizophrenia also develop delusions, but theirs differ from those that occur in paranoia in several ways. They tend to be multiple, and disconnected from each other. So, someone with schizophrenia might simultaneously believe that her parents are not her real parents, that the man next door is pumping radioactive gas in through her letter box, and that her innermost thoughts are known to the whole world.

Schizophrenic delusions also tend to be bizarre and impossible within the framework of actual reality. One of my patients believed, for example, that he had ten thousand bones in his body which migrated around while he was asleep. Another believed that his personality had shifted to his left shoulder. Compared with these, the delusional themes which occur in paranoia are usually quite convincing and entirely reasonable.

Paranoia, therefore, resembles schizophrenia in being neither recognizably organic in nature nor based on an abnormal mood. However, the only psychotic feature in paranoia is a single, delusional or hallucinatory theme. There are no other psychotic features, such as blunting of affect, formal thought disorder, or catatonia (all described in Chapter 1). The cause of paranoia can often be traced back through an already abnormal personality to a disturbed childhood. This is not true of schizophrenia. Finally, the response to treatment, particularly drug treatment, is less certain in paranoia than in schizophrenia.

Varieties of Neurosis

A neurosis is a mental illness without psychotic proportions. It is an illness, because sufferers recognize it as something alien to their normal lives over which they have no or only partial control. Even if some event did trigger it off, they recognize themselves that this cannot be the entire cause. Moreover, if the triggering event is rectified, say a broken love affair where the lover comes back, the return to a status quo is no longer sufficient to remove the neurosis. It is as if a physiological change in the brain has now been triggered, which has to run its course or be remedied with medication. Emotions which were originally reactive to the event are now autonomous and have a life and momentum of their own.

Of the five types of neuroses, only two are occasionally mistaken for schizophrenia: obsessional neurosis and hysteria. Phobias and anxiety are most unlikely to be confused with schizophrenia. In the case of depression, it is the psychotic form rather than the neurotic which is more likely to cause problems in diagnosis.

OBSESSIONAL NEUROSIS

An obsessional neurosis, or obsessive-compulsive neurosis as it is also called, is a rare mental illness in which the sufferer feels obliged to think certain thoughts – ruminations – or carry out certain actions – compulsions. The sufferer recognizes these rituals as senseless. The rituals are usually concerned with excessive cleaning, checking, repeating or avoiding things and involve, for example, checking 20 times or more that the light has been turned off, or repeated, compulsive hand-washing when the hands are perfectly clean. It affects only 1 in 2,000 of the general population, men and women equally. It is an extreme form of the way an obsessional or meticulous person approaches any task, but it reaches the stage of being an illness when the urge to carry out the rituals takes over normal activities and dominates a person's life.

Distinguishing Obsessional Neurosis from Schizophrenia

There is usually no difficulty in distinguishing an obsessional neurosis from schizophrenia because the neurotic person is only too aware of how absurd his or her behaviour is. Sufferers know that there is something the matter with them, and only wish they could return to normal. This is unlike those with schizophrenia, for whom the illness is the only reality they know. A schizophrenic's hallucinations and delusions are not absurd to him, and he does not generally remember a 'normal' world to which he wants to return. I have occasionally been referred patients with obsessional neurosis, however, because either the severity or complexity of the rituals were so marked that the referring doctor could not believe that they were simply neurotic in origin.

Richard, a young man of 22 when I saw him, had been house-bound for five years. A promising student, he had had to leave university after the first year because of an intense preoccupation with a female student, whom he had hardly spoken to. He returned to his parents and began engaging in a series of senseless and time-consuming rituals. He felt obliged to keep every cigarette end that he smoked in case there was a message in it, and any newspaper that his parents bought if the day of the week, date or month of the year had a 4 or 6 in it (e.g. Monday 13th November's could be discarded but not Thursday 14th June's). His parents had found a small piece of asbestos in the garden, which they had buried, but he became preoccupied with the possibility that his clothes were contaminated. His parents promised to pay him if he cut the lawn, but he never finished the job, because he felt he was not entitled to the money unless he cut every blade of grass individually.

Richard had consulted a psychologist on one occasion, who had tried to reorganize his thoughts into reasonable ones – for example, you don't have to cut every blade of grass – and unreasonable ones – you don't deserve any reward if you don't do the job properly. The psychologist suggested that he attribute the unreasonable, senseless thoughts to some agency outside himself and treat them as a nuisance to be overcome. Richard therefore called them 'top dog's thoughts' and was forever waging a battle in his mind between his own sensible thoughts and 'top dog's'. This actually seemed to make matters worse and the system of rituals and thoughts became so complex that several doctors wondered if he had schizophrenia, although his was, in fact, an unusually severe case of obsessional neurosis.

Philip had been diagnosed as schizophrenic at the age of 17, and was referred to me when, after four years of antischizophrenic medication, he was no better. His main problem was an inability to get out of bed before midday, and when he finally did get out of bed, even the most mundane activity such as tying his shoelaces took an immense amount of time. It was not simply an adolescent phase of lying in in the mornings, as he woke early and genuinely tried to get going. When asked why he could not do what he claimed he wanted to, or speed up simple tasks, he initially said that his body would not carry out what his mind ordered.

At first, I too considered that he might have the rare catatonic form of schizophrenia in which movements and actions become less and less spontaneous until they finally freeze altogether. But later, it became clear that the reason he found it so difficult to perform any task was that each action had to be gone over, prepared in his mind, and considered from all angles before he could do it. He was thus the slave of indecision and rumination, and not actually incapable of action as someone with catatonic schizophrenia would be. When he sat in a bath, he could not decide which part of his body to wash first, and when brushing his teeth he had to weigh up all the pros and cons of which tooth to start with. With the help of a stimulating anti-depressant and behaviour therapy (*see Chapter 6*) we managed to speed him up and virtually cure him.

Both Richard and Philip had an obsessional neurosis and not schizophrenia, because their abnormal thoughts and behaviour were based on rituals, and were not symptoms of an inexplicable change in mental functioning which is the case in schizophrenia. They were understandable and not un-understandable, which is the hallmark of schizophrenia.

HYSTERIA

The term hysteria is much misused by psychiatrists and other doctors. At worst, it is used by male doctors to describe female patients whom they do not like. At best, it refers to patients who have the symptoms of a particular illness, but who on careful investigation turn out not to have any physical evidence of the illness. So, one can have hysterical epilepsy, hysterical blindness, hysterical amnesia, hysterical paralysis, and so on.

Hysteria merges with hypochondria and is difficult to distinguish from malingering. The term hypochondria is usually reserved for people who say they are ill when they are not, whereas hysterics do not just say they are ill, they actually have all the symptoms. A malingerer is someone who actively and consciously sets out to mimic a physical illness for some ulterior motive — to avoid the duties of family life, or military service or imprisonment, for example — whereas the motivation of an hysteric is less obvious, more subconscious and certainly not actively worked out.

Distinguishing Hysteria from Schizophrenia

Most hysterics mimic physical illnesses, but they sometimes mimic mental illness, including schizophrenia. In my experience true schizophrenia is more often wrongly taken to be hysteria than the other way round, because the real symptoms of schizophrenia can be so strange that an inexperienced observer assumes they are made up. Very rarely an experienced psychiatrist is caught out diagnosing schizophrenia when it is in fact hysteria. Pamela was one such case.

She was an adopted child, and quite normal until the age of 16, when she broke her leg and was in hospital for two months. During her admission she became moderately depressed, which was an understandable and normal reaction to her situation and the fact that she was missing school which she enjoyed above everything else. On returning home she could not settle down, her school work deteriorated, and she began saying that she could see the figure of her real father, whom she had never met, pointing at her and telling her he would kill her. During the following five years she continued to see this apparition nightly. She was repeatedly admitted to a psychiatric hospital, as she had become violent towards her adoptive parents, pushing her mother through a glass door on one occasion. Apart from the apparition there were no other abnormal perceptual experiences, there were no delusions and no formal thought disorder. Her behaviour, however, became increasingly abnormal. She tried to starve herself on one occasion, and had to be admitted to an anorexia unit; she then put on an enormous amount of weight, and then started cutting her wrists and thighs.

The referring psychiatrist was at his wit's end, and described her to me as the most difficult schizophrenic that he had ever looked after. In the course of a six-month admission to my unit we gradually realized that she was not psychotic at all, and that the presence of the apparition and the self-mutilating behaviour represented her anger towards her real parents for having, as she put it, 'abandoned her to fate'. Her adoptive parents were kindly people and were bearing the brunt of Pamela's anger towards people she didn't know.

I cannot say that we cured Pamela of her underlying anger, as she continued to cut herself from time to time, but we established the correct diagnosis, and she was considerably better overall at the time of discharge than at any time in the previous five years. In particular, the apparition disappeared when we told her that we thought that she was not ill, but distressed about her unfortunate background.

There are no definite features of an hysterical condition which allow one to say with confidence that it is not the 'real thing'. Because schizophrenia can present itself in such varied ways, only an experienced psychiatrist, and one who has constant dealings with people with schizophrenia, can be expected to distinguish the two. In fact, I should admit that I too thought that Pamela was schizophrenic when I saw her in my outpatients' clinic. This shows that a careful assessment in hospital is important before making a definitive diagnosis.

The features of Pamela's condition which should have alerted me to a diagnosis of hysteria were the single hallucination

and the self-mutilating behaviour. As I have stressed, schizophrenia affects more than one aspect of the mind, and therefore the same repeated hallucination should have made me suspicious. Further, any hallucination is generally impersonal and
not a representation of some emotive preoccupation. People
with schizophrenia usually have auditory hallucinations, and if
you ask them what they are like, they say that they know they
are male or female, and remember the words, but cannot
attribute them to a known person in their lives. They virtually never have a combined visual and auditory hallucination (an
apparition they can see and hear) of someone who is known to
them or someone who is part of their background. Finally,
wrist-cutting is rare in schizophrenia. This type of behaviour
is much more common in people who wish to hurt someone
close to them. A schizophrenic's emotional life is autistic and
impersonal, and seems to preclude the sort of anger which
normal people direct at those whom they love or hate.

Varieties of Personality Disorder

There are an almost infinite number of personality traits and
therefore of personality disorders, too, because to say that
someone has a particular personality disorder only means that
one personality trait is so extreme that it causes that person to
stand out from other people because of it. However, there are
only two types of personality disorder which could possibly be
confused with schizophrenia: psychopathic personality disorder and schizoid personality disorder.

PSYCHOPATHIC PERSONALITY DISORDER
Normal people are surprised, if not appalled, that psychia-
trists do not regard all motiveless killers as schizophrenic.
How can a normal person, they argue, do something so

dreadful? – he (or she) must be mad. The answer is that the motiveless crime is usually neither committed by normal people nor by people with schizophrenia, but by people who have a particular kind of personality disorder, known as antisocial personality or psychopathic personality.

Most people commit crimes at some time in their lives. 'Middle-class' crime is by no means rare – stealing stationery from the office, using the firm's telephone for private calls or speeding on the motorway, for example. If you are brought up in a criminal fraternity in an inner suburb of a big town, crime may be regarded as fair game and entirely normal behaviour. Most of the people in our prisons are normal young men between the ages of 17 and 30 whose background has made them believe that crime is a profitable concern. Their personalities are not abnormal for their background: they are not mentally ill.

A small minority of criminals, however, do have personalities which cannot be explained in terms of the criminal ethos in which they were brought up. They do not respect family or friends as would a 'normal' criminal, who would willingly mug a rich stranger but refrain from harming an acquaintance. This type of criminal shows no remorse for his actions and seems to have no moral sense at all. They are known as psychopaths and often end up in secure institutions for the criminally insane, although they are not at all psychotic in the sense of having completely lost touch with all aspects of reality. They have no abnormal perceptions, no delusions and no formal thought disorder. Their personality has instead been damaged from an early age by parental lack of warmth, inconsistent discipline and complete failure to learn moral habits. Most of the apparently senseless crimes which have hit the newspaper headlines in the last few decades have been committed by psychopaths, and not people with schizophrenia nor by mentally well people under stress. Charles Manson, in California, and Donald Nielsen in Britain were psychopaths, not schizophrenics. Peter Sutcliffe, known as the Yorkshire Ripper, *was* schizophrenic, but he is a rare exception.

Distinguishing a Psychopath from a Schizophrenic

To make the distinction between a psychopathic personality and schizophrenia is not difficult in practice. Although the essence of schizophrenia is that it is not understandable to us, it is the schizophrenic's perceptions, thoughts and speech with which we cannot identify, not his or her behaviour. A psychopath perceives, thinks about, and talks about the world just as you and I would do. Where they differ from us is in their moral sense: they do not experience the same constraints on their actions; if they are upset or angry, for example, they can easily commit acts which you or I would find abhorrent, and they do not experience any feeling of remorse after the act.

People with schizophrenia, on the other hand, are more likely than normal people to commit a criminal act, but this is usually in response to an abnormal perception or delusion. Their intrinsic moral sense is not deranged. Peter Sutcliffe, for example, had the delusion that women, particularly prostitutes, were evil, and should be exterminated.

SCHIZOID PERSONALITY DISORDER

The only other personality disorder which can be mistaken for schizophrenia is a schizoid personality disorder. You or I know such people as eccentrics or recluses. They are not mad and not ill, but live on the edge of society, usually content with their own interests and happy provided they are not bothered. They may join or form esoteric societies with a strange religious or philosophical basis. More often they shun company, not through shyness but through a genuine sense of self-sufficiency. The trials and tribulations of life pass them by more than most people, and their lives may impinge on the rest of us only if they happen to be cantankerous neighbours or eccentric relatives.

Distinguishing Schizoid from Schizophrenic

People with a schizoid personality are at greater risk of developing a true schizophrenic illness than normal people and those with other types of abnormal personality. Some psychiatrists believe that within the schizoid personality there lie dormant the seeds of schizophrenia. Their unusual ideas about the way of the world, their self-sufficiency in their emotional life, and their peculiar way of expressing themselves are seen as the germs of delusions, blunting of affect and formal thought disorder respectively (all described in Chapter 1).

In fact, the link between a schizoid personality and schizophrenia, although genuine, is quite weak: most people with a schizoid personality will never become completely schizophrenic, and most people with schizophrenia will not have been schizoid personalities before their actual illness.

Charles is a good example of someone with a schizoid personality. I saw him at the request of a colleague in the prison service. He had assaulted another member of the religious commune in which he was living and had been arrested. He was then aged 34.

Charles was born and brought up in Dublin. His father had been the owner of a chain of newsagents and had died 10 years previously. His mother was alive and well but three of his six brothers and sisters were receiving psychiatric treatment. Charles was a normal boy and an average pupil at school. He obtained a poor degree at university and then went to Nigeria under a voluntary service scheme. He did not enjoy this and returned with the idea that he had caught a serious tropical disease, a belief which all investigations failed to confirm.

For the next four years Charles tried running a small publishing business in Dublin, but this went bankrupt. Its purpose was to promote books on vegetarianism. He became increasingly odd in his habits, disappearing without warning to live in a tent in the country and becoming fastidious about his diet. He joined an Eastern religious sect which had a commune in Ireland and another in Norfolk. He expressed no interest in sex, and all who came into contact with him pronounced him cold and aloof. He had no real friends.

He consulted a psychiatrist once because he felt anxious, but he had never experienced hallucinations and his ideas, although unusual by the standards of his background, were not firm delusions. While on a visit to the Norfolk commune he attacked another member with a piece of lead piping. The explanation for this behaviour was unclear, but he had just been asked to leave because he was not contributing to the life of the community.

When I saw him in prison he showed no sign of any mental illness but came across as someone entirely lacking in warmth and human feeling, with all the hallmarks of a schizoid personality. He was keen to talk about his religious ideas, which did not belong to any official sect, as he linked vegetarianism, physical fitness and Christianity in one confused system. I subsequently heard that he tried to secure his release from prison by

taking a priest hostage, and he was then sent to a secure
psychiatric hospital, even though he was not mentally ill.
Some psychiatrists who saw him did think he had schizophrenia, but it is very doubtful if this is true.

Normal Reaction

In these days of instant worldwide media communication, in
what sociologists have called the 'global village', we are accustomed to think that everyone is more or less like us. It is true
that the natural range of human behaviour has contracted as a
result of increased international contact between people and
by the marketing practices of big corporations projecting certain stereotypes. But there are still pockets of humanity whose
customs and beliefs have been largely uncontaminated. Even
quite sophisticated Europeans might be surprised to know that
a sizable proportion of the inhabitants of Haiti, for example,
still believe in the power of voodoo, or that 'running amok',
apparently senseless anger and violence towards neighbours
and relatives, is quite common in New Guinea in people who
feel they have been publicly insulted and humiliated. This
emphasizes the fact that madness has to be judged within a cultural setting: what may be considered madness in some cultures may be considered quite normal in others.

Even within an apparently homogeneous Western society
there are people who are otherwise quite normal in their daily
business who believe the earth is flat or that the end of the
world is upon us. We can dismiss such people as freaks or religious maniacs, but this only shows us up as narrow-minded
and unable to entertain a range of subcultural beliefs. Indeed,
many of our own beliefs, which are held by the majority of

what we assume to be reasonable-minded people, may well be regarded as quite stupid one hundred years from now. Think of the fuss about Galileo's or Darwin's discoveries.

Such considerations have a strong bearing on how we diagnose schizophrenia. Some psychiatrists and sociologists in the 1960s considered that the range of normal was so great that it was impossible, and indeed wrong, to diagnose some people as schizophrenic and others as normal. In fact, they regarded those in whom psychiatrists had identified schizophrenia to be more 'normal' in some ways than normal people. This is a ludicrous position to adopt. All societies throughout the ages have recognized madness, even though they may have treated it in different ways. The diagnosis of madness is made with respect to the individual's cultural and subcultural background, not to any absolute measure of normality. A priest's son in the 14th century who claimed that humans could travel in space would have been regarded as mad, and so would the son of an American physicist in the 1980s who suddenly developed the belief that he was an incarnated angel. Schizophrenia affects the sufferer's very ability to judge what is normal and reasonable in the social context in which we live, and it is therefore crucial to determine what the person's beliefs were before the illness began.

Finally, normal people may have strange experiences or thoughts under certain unusual circumstances. We call these dreams if we are asleep, or hypnagogic hallucinations if we are about to fall asleep. Normal people who test the limits of human endurance by sailing single-handed across the Atlantic or crossing the Arctic alone almost always report visual hallucinations, persecutory delusions or muddled thinking. This is not schizophrenia, but an early stage of delirium (described at the start of this chapter) brought about by a combination of extreme brain fatigue and sensory and social isolation.

So, behaviour that may seem really quite odd can in some circumstances be perfectly normal. This applies, as we have seen in this section, to someone who has come from a different culture to our own; to what might be called freaks or religious zealots; and to those who experience hallucinations as they are about to fall asleep.

Why We Need to Be Sure

By reading this chapter carefully you will now have an appreciation of the different types of psychiatric classifications and the 11 types of mental illness, of which schizophrenia is one. Knowing what schizophrenia is *not* is as important, if not more so, than knowing what it *is*. It should not be possible for schizophrenia to be confused, by an expert, with delirium, dementia, paranoia, phobias, anxiety, or a psychopathic personality disorder, but mistakes of this sort do, unfortunately, occur. It is easier to mistake any of the following for schizophrenia: mania, severe depression, obsessional neurosis, hysteria or a schizoid personality disorder.

Mistakes of this sort are unfortunate because schizophrenia is a condition that must be diagnosed and treated as early on in the illness as possible in order to maximize the chances of a complete recovery. If schizophrenia is allowed to persist untreated, it may gradually become more ingrained in the sufferer's personality and, therefore, perhaps more difficult to treat when it is eventually correctly diagnosed. The intention of this chapter, then, has been to give you a 'feel' for those conditions that can be mistaken for schizophrenia and an appreciation of what schizophrenia is.

3

HOW TO RECOGNIZE SCHIZOPHRENIA

Recognizing schizophrenia is fraught with difficulties even for experienced consultant psychiatrists. At the moment, diagnosis has to rely to some extent on eliminating all the other possible types of psychiatric disorders; it is crucial, therefore, to understand not only what schizophrenia is but also what it is not. This issue has been discussed at length in Chapter 2. We can now look at what could be regarded as shortcuts to diagnosis: the three rules and the first-rank symptoms described later in this chapter often prove useful in practice.

A Feel for the Problem

It is helpful for relatives and friends of someone with schizophrenia to know that there are certain typical signs of schizophrenia. (Signs, incidentally, are what an observer, such as a relative or doctor, notice; symptoms are what the patient notices.) Relatives can often give the psychiatrist valuable information about these signs, which are summarized as the three rules and the first-rank symptoms.

The diagnosis of schizophrenia is bedevilled by a number of particular problems. This chapter is intended to give you an insight into diagnosis and a 'feel' for how psychiatrists come to a definitive diagnosis.

The Principles of Diagnosis

To illustrate the general principles of how a diagnosis is made, consider first a simple illness such as appendicitis. Here there is usually one common pattern of development. It begins with pain in the central abdomen, which then gets worse and moves to the right lower abdomen. The other common causes of acute abdominal pain — say, colic, gastroenteritis and gynaecological ailments — can be systematically eliminated. In appendicitis there would be a mild fever, nausea but rarely vomiting, and constipation rather than diarrhoea. With colic there would be no fever; with gastroenteritis there would be diarrhoea and vomiting; and with gynaecological ailments a woman may have a history of menstrual problems. A diagnosis of appendicitis can never be made with absolute certainty pre-operatively, but a good doctor will know the correct series of questions to ask and physical signs to look for in order either to reduce the likelihood of an unnecessary operation or to be able to recommend an urgent one. All clinical diagnoses are made by a process of elimination, the more so in mental illness.

Difficulties in Diagnosing Schizophrenia

In tackling the problem of schizophrenia the same principles apply, but there are added complications for the psychiatrist. (Maria, in Chapter 4, offers a good example of the complexities of diagnosis.) There are at least five complicating factors:

1. The course of the illness is longer, being measured in weeks or months rather than hours. Some of the classic signs of schizophrenia, for example, are not apparent early on in the illness.

2. There is no way, at the moment, of confirming the diagnosis. There is no diseased organ to discover through surgery, and no biochemical test to rely upon, so you cannot obtain a biological confirmation of the diagnosis as in most physical illnesses, such as appendicitis or ulcer disease, for example.

3. Schizophrenia has *several* relatively common ways of beginning rather than one single way.

4. The signs and symptoms of schizophrenia are not of the same order of things as those in a physical illness such as appendicitis. Delusions and hallucinations are beliefs and experiences, respectively, and are much harder to evaluate than a tender abdomen or fever. Additionally, the signs of schizophrenia can be mistaken for signs of other mental illnesses (*see Chapter 2*).

5. The patient may not be able to help, by definition of the nature of mental illness. A mentally well person with appendicitis, for example, can remember how he or she was feeling before the pain and can describe accurately the location and intensity of the pain. People with schizophrenia can only report their new world, rather than how they saw the world before they were ill. They may not be able to observe their changed state; it is more likely that relatives and friends of the sufferer report this. The patient may not even complain of this altered state and may not want to see a doctor.

For all these reasons the diagnosis of schizophrenia has to be approached carefully and systematically.

On the positive side, however, there are considerably fewer psychiatric conditions than there are medical conditions; the six psychoses, five neuroses, personality disorder and normal reaction are all described in Chapter 2. Each of these has to be systematically eliminated, as I show in some examples in this chapter. An insight on what schizophrenia is like (*Chapter 1*) and an appreciation of what it is and what it is not (*Chapter 2*) help. You can see, nevertheless, that it is not at all easy to make an early and accurate diagnosis.

CLUES TO DIAGNOSIS: THE FIRST STEPS

Making a diagnosis of schizophrenia is, at its simplest, a matter of asking oneself systematically whether the pattern of symptoms fits schizophrenia better than any of the other psychiatric conditions. The diagnosis is hardest of all at an early stage because the most typical symptoms take longer to appear, and those that do appear at the beginning are usually vague and non-specific. The two main ways in which the illness may show itself are: as an acute florid (very noticeable) change in behaviour over a matter of weeks, usually constituting a crisis in the sufferer's family or circle of friends; or as a gradual deterioration in personality over months or years.

Sudden Changes in Behaviour

Elena is a good example of the acute, or comparatively sudden development of schizophrenia. She was 37 when she was first admitted to a psychiatric hospital. She came from a professional family, went to university, and then entered the Foreign Office. Her work there was quite exemplary and she was promoted to commercial attaché in a South American embassy. She had never married but had had several close relationships with men. She was normal in all respects until her breakdown in Peru. The circumstances and details of what happened there are unclear to me even to this day, possibly because the Foreign Office were themselves reluctant to divulge information. She was flown back to Britain, however, and admitted to our hospital. All we could discover was that she had developed persecutory ideas concerning a local Peruvian who had some dealings with the Embassy. The embassy doctor had then prescribed large doses of an antischizophrenic drug, and when she arrived in our ward she was heavily tranquillized.

The political situation in Peru at the time was tense, and it seemed to me that there might well be good reasons for an embassy official to feel suspicious of the locals. Elena herself did not help our investigations by remaining silent about her experiences abroad, whether through embarrassment or adherence to diplomatic secrecy I never knew.

In the first few weeks of admission, however, Elena appeared free of any gross mental disturbance in the form of hallucinations, delusions or formal thought disorder. Her behaviour in the ward was unusual for a diplomat, in that she developed a passion for a male nurse and several male patients, but this could be due to a high sexual drive and was certainly not evidence of a psychosis.

At this point the diagnosis was uncertain. I went systematically in my mind through the possibilities (the 4 Levels of psychiatric classification – *see pages 26–27*). I started with the most 'normal' explanations first:

1. Could this have been a *normal reaction* to intolerable stress in a difficult job far away from home without the support of family and friends?

   This seemed to me a distinct possibility, particularly since we had so little evidence of psychotic features other than persecutory ideas.

2. Did she have a *personality disorder* which made her respond to normal events in an exaggerated way?

   We interviewed several family members, who all said that Elena was a pretty normal person before going to Peru, and so this possibility could be eliminated.

3. What about a *neurosis*?

   Elena was neither depressed nor anxious in mood, and had no obsessions or phobias. Hysteria could also be ruled out because she was at pains to play down the episode in South America and wished only to return to work as quickly as possible.

4. Of the different varieties of *psychosis* which Elena could be suffering from, we first considered an acute organic psychosis. She was physically healthy but could conceivably have been an alcoholic or drug addict. Her relatives dismissed this suggestion. The acute onset precluded the possibility of dementia. She was not depressed and, apart from her inappropriate sexual behaviour, there was no sign of mania.

We were left then with three possibilities – a normal reaction to a stressful life situation, paranoia or schizophrenia.

I stopped Elena's antischizophrenic drugs as I felt they were aggravating the diagnostic problem. I reasoned that if she only had a stress reaction she would not need medication now that she was removed from the stressful environment, and that the drugs may have been masking her true mental state. If she did have paranoia or schizophrenia then this would reappear in time. Stopping the antischizophrenic drugs was thus a diagnostic test. The pattern of her relapse, if it occurred, would allow one to distinguish between these two.

There was another reason for stopping the drugs. I believe that someone with schizophrenia usually responds well to the correct medication and should stay on it for the foreseeable future. It is therefore crucial, in my view, to establish the diagnosis once and for all at the start. Otherwise, a person suffering from another condition could be given the wrong medication, unnecessarily, for years. Equally, someone with schizophrenia may be denied the benefits of the correct treatment.

For three weeks after her medication was stopped Elena remained the same. However, one weekend she set off by train to visit a cousin who lived on the other side of London. She arrived back on the ward late that night without having got there. She had become totally lost on the journey because everything, including stations she knew well, suddenly seemed unfamiliar. Everyone on the train, she said, had been looking at her in a strange way and conversing among themselves in a language she had never heard before. Although this was conceivably true, it was rather unlikely as it was a quiet suburban line. The most telling evidence that she had suffered a return of abnormal perceptual experiences was her further comment that everyone appeared to be talking in a 'high, shrill and eerie way'. I was now convinced we had established the diagnosis of schizophrenia: Elena's perceptual experiences were quite typical (*see Perceptual Disorder in Chapter 1*); she did not have the single delusional theme characteristic of paranoia (demonstrated by Louise in Chapter 2); and what she was experiencing could no longer be regarded as a normal stress reaction. We restarted her medication and she has remained well ever since.

The onset of William's illness illustrates the problem of distinguishing schizophrenia from manic and depressive psychoses. He was 16 when first admitted to a psychiatric hospital. He had left school six months previously and had started work as a trainee in a men's outfitters. His parents had separated when he was 13 and he now lived with his father and elder brother, though he had regular contact with his mother. He had not appeared particularly distressed at the family break-up. William was described as rather a loner in his last years at school, having only one friend, but always seemed happy with his three main hobbies – studying horse-racing form, keeping fit and reading books on psychology. He had shown no interest in girls.

There was no indication of anything seriously wrong with him until five weeks before his admission to hospital. At this point his behaviour changed. From being enthusiastic about his job he now sat in a daze all day and was eventually given the sack. He began taking midnight walks, usually to the local branch of the Midland Bank, where he would stand outside for hours looking desolate, and was once picked up by the police for acting suspiciously. He later explained this behaviour by saying that he had fallen in love with a bank clerk there, and could not get her out of his mind. In fact, he had only seen her once. He discovered her name, and would write it all over his books. He even circled with hearts the entry in the telephone directory of the local branch of the bank. He became rude to his father, something which was totally out of character, and neglected his appearance. The day before admission he mentioned to his father that he thought his room was bugged and that he himself was God.

For the first week in hospital William was assessed without medication. His mood fluctuated wildly: one moment he would be found slumped dejectedly in the toilet, another he would be pacing up and down in extreme agitation, yet another he would be seen rolling on the floor 'in ecstasy', as he said, at the thought of the bank clerk Miss X. He spoke in a peculiar way, with a pseudo-American accent, which his father said was quite new, and with the occasional use of odd abbreviations — for example, 'secs' for seconds, when this was out of place. He was preoccupied with Miss X, saying 'I don't feel good enough for her,' 'She makes me guilty' and once 'Look what love's done to me.' He denied hearing voices or seeing the world in a strange way, but did appear to have abnormal bodily sensations, commenting that he felt that blood was rushing from his brain to his heart and that he was being turned into a monkey. He also believed, though seemed uncertain about how this came about, that his 'life was being looked into' and that he was 'being listened to'.

Tackling the diagnosis systematically as before, the first question which arose was whether William's behaviour was normal or not. Some of his behaviour and preoccupations could have been adolescent or indeed a consequence of any sort of intense love. The fact that he had only seen Miss X once and had not even spoken to her was neither here nor there.

1. Was he then just madly in love, as it were, a *normal reaction*?

   This was an inadequate explanation, because there were other strange thoughts and experiences that had nothing to do with being in love — feeling that he was being turned into a monkey or listened to, for example.

2. Although he was rather a loner at school and his collection of interests might appear rather unusual, one cannot correctly say that he had a *personality disorder* because he was too young to have developed an adult personality. Moreover, his ideas and experiences had gone beyond the bounds of normality, and had reached psychotic proportions. Whether his personality was abnormal or not, his present state could not be entirely explained in this way.

3. His psychotic state excluded the possibility of *neurosis*.

4. Considering now the various types of *psychosis*, there was no evidence of any illicit drug-taking and this, along with negative investigations for physical illness, eliminated the

possibility of an acute organic psychosis. The question of dementia did not arise because his symptoms began so abruptly. The possibility of this being a depressive psychosis or mania, however, had to be considered. Certainly his mood was abnormal though there was no single prevailing mood: sometimes he was elated, sometimes depressed. Ideas were at times consistent with either a low mood – that he felt guilty or not good enough for Miss X; or a high mood – that he was God. However, taking the clinical picture as a whole, not all William's ideas, experiences and behaviour could be said to stem from his change in mood. His belief that he was being turned into a monkey, for example, is incongruent with (not to do with) any mood. For this reason, his illness could not be regarded as a form of affective psychosis (*see pages 26–27*). Neither was it a form of paranoia, because there were several independent delusional themes as well as abnormalities in his speech (the pseudo-American accent), and in the form in which he expressed his thoughts (the odd use of abbreviations).

For all these reasons a diagnosis of schizophrenia was more or less certain, and William was started on antischizophrenic medication. This was many years ago when I was a junior doctor and I lost track of him when I moved to a different hospital. I heard subsequently that he had committed suicide, which is a genuine tragedy and waste. It shows, however, how frightening and potentially fatal the symptoms of schizophrenia can be.

Elena and William illustrate some of the different ways in which schizophrenia can affect previously normal people. In Elena's case it happened in her middle thirties, by which time she was already a mature person and able to compensate for and then adapt to a psychotic episode in her life. In William's case it occurred at the very age when he was trying to understand himself and come to terms with his background. For this reason it had a more devastating effect on him. This is often the tragedy of schizophrenia, that it affects people at the most vulnerable period of their lives, when they are changing from adolescence into adulthood.

Gradual Deterioration

Schizophrenia can also develop slowly and be hard to distinguish from someone who already has a personality disorder. Jonathan was such a case.

Jonathan was born and brought up in Australia. His father was a journalist and his mother a librarian. He had five brothers and sisters, one of whom was a heroin addict and one who had been diagnosed as schizophrenic. At school he was considered an above-average pupil until the age of 16, when he lost all interest in academic work.

He first became noticeably unwell at the age of 17, soon after a chest infection. He became listless, rarely got out of bed till the afternoon and stopped speaking to his family. This was initially put down to glandular fever, although there was no laboratory confirmation of this. His parents moved to England at this time and he stayed with an aunt. His behaviour was then attributed to his missing his parents. He joined his parents in London and enrolled for a higher education course but dropped out after six weeks. He returned to Australia and at his parents' suggestion lived with some cousins on their farm. This, too, was a failure as he annoyed them with such behaviour as driving their car with no lights on in the middle of the night. Occasionally he would say strange things, for example once saying, à propos of nothing, 'It's no good. I'm going mad.'

I saw Jonathan soon after he had returned to London for the second time. It was then seven years since he had dropped out of school and six since his listlessness was noticed. The visit was precipitated by an unprovoked episode of violence towards his father. He had broken his father's radio and thrown his work papers around the room, and when asked to explain this had punched his father repeatedly in the face. In the few weeks since his arrival from Australia there had been other inexplicable incidents – he had smashed up his guitar because he said it made his ears buzz, he had walked away from the television in a very agitated way and had shouted out of the window to nobody, 'Go away and leave me alone.'

He was admitted to hospital after a visit by the family's general practitioner. This doctor, unfortunately, gave him an injection of a long-acting antischizophrenic drug and for the first six weeks in the ward Jonathan denied any unusual experiences or beliefs, and apart from appearing totally unconcerned about his situation there was nothing out of the ordinary in his behaviour.

After six weeks he was clamouring to be discharged. His parents were also concerned that I had not made a definitive diagnosis. By this time, luckily, the effect of the long-acting medication was wearing off. I remember vividly that just as I was agreeing to discharge him, convinced that I could not be sure of the diagnosis, I asked if there was anything he wanted to tell me before he went. Jonathan replied, 'Yes. My brain is turning round. It is circling round inside my head.' He was not just joking; he actually believed it. And, during the next week Jonathan admitted other strange ideas and experiences — for example, that his left arm was ballooning out, that his father had sexually molested him when he was four and that he could hear people whispering about his internal thoughts.

Unfortunately, Jonathan discharged himself against our advice at this point and then returned to Australia. It had taken a long time to make a diagnosis. We would have come to a more speedy conclusion but for the fact that he had been given a long-acting injection by his general practitioner. The importance of correct diagnosis, however, perhaps carrying with it lifelong medication, is so important that six weeks of assessment is trivial compared with the long-term issues involved.

Jonathan's case illustrates well the problem of how a series of strange incidents in someone's behaviour can be passed off as due to unusual circumstances or adolescent 'high jinks'. It was only when I was convinced beyond doubt that he had the characteristic features of schizophrenia that I was prepared to make a definitive diagnosis.

DELAY IN DIAGNOSIS

Relatives often criticize psychiatrists for being too cautious in making the diagnosis, and for allowing mayhem to occur before admitting the sufferer to hospital and relieving the family. To some extent this is the fault of Britain's current Mental Health legislation, which makes it very difficult to admit and treat people without their agreement. It is also a genuine desire by most psychiatrists to put off the moment when they make the actual diagnosis of schizophrenia. In the old days, before effective treatment, this was understandable because it was virtually a sentence of lifelong hospitalization. Now it is anything but that, in fact the opposite: a correct diagnosis followed by correct treatment leads to a marked improvement in 80–90 per cent of people with schizophrenia; any unnecessary delay would be foolhardy. Equally, however, any error in diagnosis, in either direction – schizophrenia for some other illness or some other illness for schizophrenia – could be disastrous, even fatal.

What to Look for as a Relative or Friend

Because schizophrenia involves a change from one state of mind to another, only a close observer – such as a relative or friend – can judge whether a change in ideas is totally out of character or whether it is a natural progression of latent personality traits. Psychiatrists, although they may deny it, are almost completely dependent on an informant for this information. However, if the sufferer has delusions that go beyond the realms of what is true of the natural world then a diagnosis can be made with more certainty. This is borne out in many of the case histories I have quoted in this chapter and Chapters 1 and 2. If someone says that she came down from Mars on a ray of light the diagnosis is clear-cut. If she says, as one of my West Indian patients did, that the Prime Minister of St Lucia visited her in London every weekend, then this is very unlikely, but just about plausible, and has to be confirmed or refuted. If she says that a Peruvian diplomat was spying on them, as Elena (described earlier in this chapter) did, this requires careful investigation to tease out what is true from what is false.

First rule – complete lack of common sense about
the way the world is.

The first rule, therefore, is to look for what is totally outside
the bounds of possibility in the sufferer's ideas.

Dennis had been an in-patient in the long-stay ward of a
psychiatric hospital for 18 years when I first met him. I
asked him what had been wrong with him all these years
and he told me that he had had pneumonia all this time.
I commented that it was a long time to have had pneumonia. He said that he had caught it from a thermome-
ter at Guy's Hospital in London on which was written
that everyone would either get 'flu or pneumonia and he
had got the pneumonia. I pointed out that thermometers
only measure temperature, they do not specify what illnesses people get. He retorted 'You'd better go back and
look up your medical books' and then walked out of the
room.

Dennis showed a complete absence of common sense
or judgement about what thermometers do and knew
even less than the least intelligent person about illness.
He was not unintelligent, in fact, as he was training to be
a barrister when he first became ill.

A patient interviewed by Roger Brown, professor of psychology at Harvard University, also illustrates the rule about lack
of common sense, but shows how the ideas involved may not
be so absurd. Professor Brown's patient was asked what he

planned to do on leaving hospital. He replied that he intended to go to Scotland to audition for a star part in the film *Fiddler on the Roof*. This is superficially quite plausible until one realizes that the film had already been made, that Scotland was an odd location for a film about traditional Jewish customs and that he was the wrong age for the part.

> Second rule – a dramatic and, to us, incomprehensible change in the way the world is experienced.

People with schizophrenia have experiences which no one else has, even under the most extreme conditions imaginable. They hear voices discussing among themselves their most intimate thoughts or they hear their thoughts echoed aloud or they see the world fragmented until the entire balance between foreground and background, detail and context, is totally changed. At the height of such experiences someone with schizophrenia is rarely able to explain to you that this is what is happening. You have to deduce this from what the person does or says.

In the same way as sufferers may suddenly reveal *an absurd idea*, they sometimes tell you about an *experience which is so incomprehensible* that the diagnosis is clear. You would otherwise have to build up a picture of what you suspect that they are experiencing.

Daniel, a classics scholar, explained his experiences in a way which is unmistakable:

I hear two voices when I am alone. One is a man's, the other a woman's. They refer to me in what is in grammatical terms the third person. In Latin the word *amo* – I love – is the first person singular of the verb, *amas* – you love – is the second person singular, and *amat* – he, she or it loves – is the third person singular. The voices I hear are always in the third person 'He is walking to the shops' or 'He is thinking rude thoughts.'

More often than not one can only suspect, though often with some degree of confidence, that someone is hallucinating or perceiving the world in a bizarre way. Jonathan, the Australian patient, was almost certainly experiencing auditory hallucinations and visual or auditory distortions before his admission. He shouted out of the window when nobody was around, 'Go away and leave me alone,' and became visibly upset or aggressive towards any machine which made a noise or broadcast speech – his guitar, the radio and the television.

> Third rule – an inexplicable change in the way emotions, speech or movement are expressed.

The final set of observations that can assist in establishing the diagnosis is to look for the peculiar and characteristic way in which people with schizophrenia express themselves. It is not so much *what* they feel, say or do that is the key, because people with any psychiatric illness will say odd things, feel differently from normal and behave out of character. What distinguishes schizophrenia from all other mental illnesses is *how* sufferers show their emotions, speak or act.

We saw that William began talking with a pseudo-American accent and used abbreviations when these were out of place. In Chapter 1, I gave examples of the way people with schizophrenia, in their conversation and writings, take no account of the conventions which a listener or reader needs to be able to follow their train of thoughts. It is this total transformation of language itself – a new accent, new words, new turns of phrase – which is characteristic.

Their emotional life, too, is transformed, but our only windows on it – facial expression, gesture, the words they use – are themselves distorted. It is as if we were trying to follow a medieval Japanese play, for example, with both language and customs that are new to us, with the additional disadvantage of seeing it through distorting spectacles. Nothing is what it seems. People with schizophrenia may giggle to themselves or show anger over some trivial incident or appear blank. We do not know if they have found something we've said funny or irritating or boring. The answer usually is that it is none of these, but that their emotional responses have become divorced from whatever they are feeling. Trudy, one of my patients, would giggle away throughout an entire half-hour interview, but it had no quality of embarrassment about it, and no infectious quality which an adolescent girl's would have. Rather, it was empty of feeling, and she would often switch to intense anger without warning.

The actions and posture of schizophrenics are also subject to an internal disorganization which usually has nothing to do either with what is going on around them or with their intentions. Sam, another patient, would stand motionless for hours on the pavement outside his college, and in hospital showed an extreme hesitation in everything he did. Entering a room he would stand transfixed at every step, as if his will to act had been frozen.

Mark's behaviour, for example, was intensely annoying and contrary, as whatever you asked him to do he would do the opposite. When you gave up trying to persuade him and walked off, he would then immediately do what it was you had originally wanted. Most people saw this as pure bloody-mindedness, but he did it so regularly, regardless of the circumstances, that it was clearly out of his control, and was what is known as *negativism*.

As normal people, we are accustomed to look for reasons even for the most outlandish behaviour. And this is right. For much of the time people with schizophrenia do maintain some contact with reality. They show normal embarrassment or anger, and can purposely be a nuisance, just like anyone else. The key to their condition, however, is that sometimes their emotions, speech or actions betray the fact that their control over these matters is limited and shaky. Parts of themselves, as it were, become split off from the mainstream and take on a will of their own. This is exactly what the word schizophrenia means. It doesn't mean so much split personality as split mind. The various parts of the mind are no longer co-ordinated either between themselves or within each function itself.

What we as observers notice, however, is a series of unusual incidents. At first we find unusual explanations to match the unusual behaviour. But as time goes on and more and more incidents occur, with no particular pattern to them, we gradually run out of explanations. It is at this point that we concede defeat and admit that the person's behaviour no longer accords with even a liberal interpretation of normality. This is the point when we can no longer communicate effectively with the person and decide that he or she must be ill.

What Psychiatrists Place Most Weight On

Unfortunately, psychiatrists disagree more about schizophrenia than any other condition. I have often been called in by solicitors to see someone in prison who the prison psychiatrist has said is a normal (mentally well) criminal, only to discover that the person is profoundly psychotic and almost certainly suffering from schizophrenia.

You, as relatives or friends, may be perplexed or even annoyed at the diversity of opinion among psychiatrists who have looked after your relative. It would require another book in itself to uncover the reasons for this (I have made an attempt to do this in a previous book, *The Psychology of Schizophrenia*). The problem is that, because there is no certain way of proving the diagnosis, each psychiatrist feels at liberty to diagnose schizophrenia in whatever way he or she pleases. Although most of them would probably not disagree with the three rules given above, they would interpret them differently and add additional rules, each according to what he or she had been taught as a trainee psychiatrist.

I hope in this book to give you enough information for you to feel fairly confident in your *own* diagnostic abilities. If a psychiatrist tells you, for example, that your sister has schizophrenia, or more likely does not, you will have the knowledge to judge this on its own merits. Gone are the days when a doctor's or indeed any professional person's opinion is accepted without reservation. We all want to be part of important decisions. I do, when it comes to my children's education or damp-proofing the house. Schizophrenia is mysterious, certainly, but it can be tackled with the same logic and common sense as any other problem.

The most constructive conversation I have had about schizophrenia in recent years was with the father of a schizophrenic man. He was a solicitor, and weighed his words carefully. He had lived with his son's illness for eight years, had been through 15 psychiatrists and knew the Mental Health Act inside out. He had never heard of Emil Kraepelin, Eugen Bleuler or other eminent psychiatrists, but he had a logical person's ability to know what was sensible and what not. Unfortunately, some psychiatrists approach diagnosis in a very narrow-minded way. They look for the signs and symptoms of the condition as if they were as simple as fever or a tender abdomen.

First-rank Symptoms

Without going into all the ins and outs of what psychiatrists do or don't believe, you should know that in most English-speaking countries these days the main diagnostic guidelines are those laid down by German psychiatrist Kurt Schneider just after the Second World War. Schneider described 11 types of what he called first-rank symptoms; these have come to be recognized as important guidelines to diagnosis.

THE FIRST-RANK SYMPTOMS
- 1.–3. Three sorts of auditory hallucinations
- 4.–6. Three sorts of ideas about one's thoughts not being one's own
- 7.–10. Four sorts of ideas about other aspects of oneself not being one's own and being controlled
- 11. One type of delusion based on an altered perception of the world

In short, the first-rank symptoms are a collection of different types of auditory hallucinations and delusions (*see list of Schneider's First-rank Symptoms, below*). Schneider did not mention the peculiar quality of sufferers' speech, emotional responses or actions, but most psychiatrists would add these to their list of typical symptoms. I myself think that the usefulness of these first-rank symptoms has been overrated, but I accept that most people with schizophrenia, whatever the precise diagnostic rules one uses, will experience one or more of them at some stage of their illness.

SCHNEIDER'S FIRST-RANK SYMPTOMS

Hearing voices

1. Audible thoughts – Voices speaking thoughts aloud
2. Voices arguing – Two or more hallucinatory voices discussing the sufferer in the third person, referring to the sufferer as 'he', 'she' or 'it'
3. Voices commenting on one's action – Voices describing sufferer's activities as they occur

Thoughts not being one's own

4. Thought withdrawal – Sufferer believes thoughts are removed from his head
5. Thought insertion – Thoughts have quality of not being one's own, ascribed to external agency
6. Thought broadcasting – Thoughts experienced as escaping into the outside world, and known to others

Outside forces

7. Influence playing on the body – Experience of bodily sensations by external agency, such as a tingling in the legs caused by electric current
8. Imposed feelings – Feelings do not seem to be one's own,

attributed to an external force

9. Imposed impulses – Drive or impulse seems to be alien and external – an alien force directing one's will

10. Imposed actions – Actions and movements felt to be under outside control; an alien force directing one's actions

Delusion

11. Delusional perception – Completely illogical conclusion drawn from a perceptual experience, for example, when seeing a cat cross the road the sufferer concludes that the end of the world is at hand

Most psychiatrists, as I said, rely mainly on Schneider's first-rank symptoms, but if these are not present they then pay attention to whether there are other *specific* symptoms such as formal thought disorder, blunting or inappropriate affect and catatonia (all of which are described in Chapter 1).

OTHER COMMON SYMPTOMS

At various times in their illness people with schizophrenia may show all sorts of delusions and hallucinations – not just the more characteristic ones I have picked out. The most common non-specific delusions are probably persecutory delusions – believing someone or some persons are out to harm or kill you; and delusions about bodily change – that parts of oneself are changing shape, size or position. Similarly, schizophrenics experience hallucinations in every sense, not just hearing. They may taste, smell, see or feel a variety of odd experiences.

WHAT'S NORMAL

Psychiatrists also place some weight on what remains normal in someone who has schizophrenia. A schizophrenic can still do some things perfectly well, showing that some parts of the brain are unaffected. The normal part of the mind, however, is subverted to the abnormal part of the mind, even though the normal parts retain their individual integrity. For example, an outstanding musician could still play his instrument technically superbly but with little emotional quality; the musician might at the same time be hearing voices and imagining commands – but his playing may remain unimpaired.

As another example, Peter Sutcliffe (the Yorkshire Ripper) was able to live an organized life and plan each murder meticulously and ruthlessly, yet he too showed some of the classic signs of schizophrenia (*see also page 59*). A deluded person, therefore, may still be able to perform some tasks efficiently.

People with schizophrenia vary in how much they are divorced from reality. Those whose grip upon reality is still strong are those most likely to commit crimes, because they have enough common sense left in one part of their mind to carry out what the deluded part of their mind drives them to.

Characteristically, there is nothing wrong with a schizophrenic's memory or concentration. Their ability to think logically is often normal, too: most of their delusions stem more from trying to make sense to themselves of their bizarre perceptual experiences than from any impairment in general logic. Also, in most areas of perception (except those discussed in Chapter 1), they do not differ from the rest of us. And this strange transformation in their perception of space and how things fit together is often very short-lived. By the time a psychiatrist sees them this stage may have passed and have given way to firm delusions.

DETERIORATION OF THE PERSONALITY

Many psychiatrists believe that schizophrenia causes an *irreversible change* in someone's personality even if the delusions, hallucinations and other symptoms clear up with medication. A minority of sufferers, it is true, become more unsociable, less inclined to look for work and develop interests which they did not have before. This change in personality, however, is by no means inevitable.

As a relative or friend, you may well notice this change and help the psychiatrist towards a diagnosis, since only you will know what the person was like before the onset of the illness.

Coming to a Final Diagnosis

Diagnosis rests upon a change between one state and another. The only people that can really tell are the relatives – the patient often cannot, because he is isolated in his new world. A psychiatrist cannot, because he did not see the sufferer when he was well. The information that relatives can give is, therefore, crucial.

RELUCTANCE TO RECOGNIZE THE ILLNESS

There are a number of reasons a the psychiatrist may be reluctant to offer a firm diagnosis of schizophrenia. These include:

1. He or she will wish to be sure that the diagnosis is certain, for the reasons stated at the start of this chapter and for the reasons stated under Delay in Diagnosis, above.

2. The label schizophrenia has a number of consequences for a person's life. A psychiatrist must feel confident, therefore, before he or she attaches this label, that it is the correct one. For example, I know of several medical students whose future career was stopped short once they were

diagnosed as schizophrenic, because the Dean of their medical school observed a rule that no student diagnosed with schizophrenia should be allowed to progress to becoming a fully qualified doctor.

3. Some psychologists and a few psychiatrists have been reluctant to accept the concept of mental illness at all (discussed in Chapter 2) and would therefore not make a diagnosis of schizophrenia. This is unfortunate, as it means that people with schizophrenia will be offered inappropriate therapies and will be denied the chance of effective drug treatment.

CONFIRMATION OF DIAGNOSIS

I hope that this chapter will have given you some insights and sufficient information, particularly when read in conjunction with Chapters 1 and 2, to help you feel confident of a diagnosis and to ask the right questions. If a psychiatrist makes a diagnosis you feel to be incorrect, ask for a second opinion through your general practitioner. (Obtaining a second opinion is discussed in Chapter 7, under Concern about Diagnosis.) The sooner the correct diagnosis is established, the sooner the appropriate treatment can commence.

4

WHO DEVELOPS SCHIZOPHRENIA?

Worldwide, 1 in 100 people develops schizophrenia at some time in life. This means that in Great Britain, for example, with a population of 60 million, there are over 500,000 people alive now who will have, or have had, schizophrenia.

This makes the illness relatively common, more so than, say, multiple sclerosis or Parkinson's disease, which receive much more publicity. It is not the most common mental illness, however. Over a lifetime, 1 in 10 people experiences a depressive neurosis or psychosis, 1 in 20 an anxiety neurosis, and 1 in 30 a phobic neurosis (*see Chapter 2*). Schizophrenia is in some ways worse than any of these, however, because if it is not properly treated it will almost certainly continue to affect someone's well-being for the rest of his or her life. Depressive, anxiety and phobic illnesses nearly always clear up on their own, regardless of treatment.

This bare figure of 1 in 100, however, conceals the fact that the risk of developing schizophrenia is not the same for everyone. Some people have a higher risk than others. These 'risk factors' are what this chapter is about — pointing out which sorts of people are more likely than the average to develop schizophrenia.

The importance of knowing such facts is twofold. First, it helps the relatives of a person with schizophrenia to appreciate what risks they themselves or other family members have of developing the condition. Secondly, it provides researchers working to find the cause of schizophrenia with crucial evidence to support or refute a particular theory about the *cause* of schizophrenia.

What Is Meant by 'Risk Factors'?

Virtually all illnesses, even those with a clear-cut cause such as tuberculosis (caused by a species of bacteria known as the tubercle bacillus), do not affect everyone who comes into contact with the causal agent. Who gets tuberculosis, for example, depends on the age of the person, where he lives and his general level of nutrition, among other factors. Even at the peak of tuberculosis in Europe, in the early part of the 20th century, some people with all the odds stacked against them – living with an infected relative, right age, poor nutritional status – escaped the illness. These people had some protective factor, presumably in the strength of their immune systems, which combated the infection.

In the case of schizophrenia, although its exact cause is not known with anything like the degree of certainty (*see Chapter 5*) as is true of tuberculosis, it is still possible to identify risk factors.

These risk factors, which have a definite bearing on the development of schizophrenia, include:

- age
- gender
- genetic make-up (inherited from the family)
- childhood character and adult personality.

There are other *possible* risk factors, which are still being scientifically evaluated, but you should be aware of the evidence for and against these as they are occasionally mentioned in books and articles about schizophrenia. These include:

• race and geographical location
• mild degrees of brain damage, most often incurred before, during or just after birth.

Finally, there are certain factors which were once thought to be important but are now *definitely ruled out*. Again, it is worth being aware of these, as they are still mentioned in some books and articles about schizophrenia. They include certain child-rearing practices, stress and certain dietary patterns.

Definite Risk Factors

THE AGE FACTOR
Most people with schizophrenia show the first symptoms of their illness during late adolescence or early adulthood. The peak period for men is between the ages of 16 and 26; for women, between 26 and 36. This pattern is different from that of any other mental illness. The risk of developing a depressive illness, for example, remains constant throughout adulthood: it is not at all uncommon for people in their seventies or eighties to have their first episode of a depressive illness. Anxiety and phobic neuroses are most common in either sex in the late twenties and early thirties. Dementia rarely begins before the age of 65, and the risk of developing it increases substantially thereafter.

Typical Age of Onset

A typical development is the case of a boy who has been quite normal until his late teens and then, unexpectedly, does very badly in his school-leaving exams. This is not to say that any boy who gives up or fails in his academic studies has schizophrenia. Far from it. The hallmark of the condition is behaviour, thoughts and reported experiences which are totally incomprehensible. But, if a previously intelligent and 'normal' child repeatedly does or says things which are totally unexpected, then a diagnosis of schizophrenia should be considered.

Ian's case illustrates this pattern. Ian was the only son of two doctors and lived in a seaside town on the south coast of England. He was a sociable child and did well at his primary school. In the first five years at secondary school he was regarded as one of the cleverest boys in his class. He passed nine '0' level exams at the age of 16 with excellent grades and was expected to have no trouble with his university entrance exams. But from then on he showed no further interest in his studies. He would wander off in the middle of the day and would be seen sitting on the beach, staring out to sea. He later went to a technical college and scraped enough grades to get to university. He then dropped out of this course after a few weeks and worked as a deck-chair attendant in his home town. After several inexplicable attacks on his father, whom he accused of having inserted a microchip in his ear, he was admitted to hospital where the characteristic features of schizophrenia were observed.

Early-onset Schizophrenia

It is very rare for anyone under the age of 16 to show signs of schizophrenia. Occasionally, however, this does happen, in which case the condition is known as childhood schizophrenia. It is particularly difficult to recognize, because some of the characteristic delusions and hallucinations – the first-rank symptoms (*see Chapter 3*) – may not be present, and strange behaviour may be the chief feature, for which reason the illness is often mistaken for mere 'naughtiness' or adolescent turmoil.

Some psychiatrists, myself included, believe that the condition known as autism, in which a child never develops normal social behaviour but may be intellectually bright, is the very earliest way that schizophrenia can develop. There are several differences, however, between autism and even childhood schizophrenia, and most child psychiatrists regard the two as different illnesses.

Late-onset Schizophrenia

Although it is rare for schizophrenia to begin for the first time after the age of 40, it does happen, particularly in women. It is usually milder in degree at this age, and particularly difficult to diagnose because many of the characteristic features of schizophrenia are absent.

One of my patients, Maria, illustrates the problem. She was 65 years old when I was first called to see her, at her home. She was Italian and her husband was Polish and neither spoke much English. They mainly communicated through their daughter, who knew both languages as well as English. They had both come to England soon after the Second World War. Maria had worked in a biscuit factory until retiring two years previously.

The immediate problem was that she had developed the belief that her husband was ganging up with a neighbour to steal her pension book. She had taken to locking him out of the house, and he had called their doctor, who then called me. It was difficult to understand what was going on in her mind because of the language problem, so I suggested she come into hospital for a fuller assessment. She refused, but two weeks later she took an overdose of tablets, was admitted to a general hospital to have her stomach washed out, and then reluctantly agreed to be transferred to us.

There were a number of problems to sort out before we could arrive at a diagnosis. First, we had to find out what she had been like in her earlier years. She had never had a serious breakdown requiring hospital admission before, but her daughter told us that for as long as she could remember, and she was now 28, her mother had been a difficult and suspicious person. She would not let her daughter bring her friends to the house and often refused to let her daughter go to school in case 'something happened'. Her present concern about the neighbour and her husband had been building up for five years. It now looked as if her condition was more long-standing than it at first appeared.

Secondly, she had suffered diabetes and thyroid disease for over 10 years and, although she was supposed to be on tablets for these conditions, she had not been taking them regularly. It could have been, therefore, that her psychiatric state was an organic psychosis (*see pages*

26–27) that had its origins in either diabetic or thyroid disturbance of the brain.

Thirdly, when the psychologist in our team tested her intelligence and memory – something we tend to do if there is a question of organic brain disease – it was found that her IQ was borderline subnormal. This raised the question of whether she had always been rather dull or whether this was a recent deterioration, suggesting the start of dementia.

Finally, I wondered if she were depressed, because although she would not say much about her feelings, she looked sad most of the time, she was always sighing, she had taken an overdose and she occasionally remarked mournfully that she had been a good person all her life, suggesting she might have some delusions of guilt.

Over a period of weeks, we eventually teased out these problems. We stabilized her diabetes and thyroid disease and corrected an anaemia that we had found. All this had no effect on her mental state. We carried out a brain scan, which was normal. If she had had dementia, the scan would have shown a thinning of the brain surface, which it didn't. Her mood improved on the ward, whereas her delusions increased – she attacked a nurse who she thought was referring to her as a prostitute, and threw some boiling water over another patient who she thought was trying to kill her. This eliminated a depressive psychosis as a possibility. She was not an obvious case of paranoia because there were several *unconnected* delusional themes. We concluded, therefore, that she had a late schizophrenia, or *paraphrenia* as it is sometimes called, which to our delight improved considerably with an antischizophrenic drug. She was later able to return home to a reasonably settled life.

GENDER AS A RISK FACTOR

The overall risk of developing schizophrenia at some time in our lives is the same for men as for women, so it cannot strictly be said that being male or female is a risk factor. However, the peak period for men is younger than for women. The average age of onset in men is 24, in women it is 30. There are other differences between the sexes, too. Men generally have a more severe form of the illness and are less likely to make a full recovery. In the days before effective treatment, for example, there were three times as many men as women in the long-stay wards of mental hospitals. There are also differences in the signs of schizophrenia between men and women. Men, for example, have more formal thought disorder and blunting of affect (described in Chapter 1), whereas women are more likely to have delusions. So, being male or female certainly has an influence on when the illness starts, what form it takes, and how it develops. In that sense, it is a risk factor.

These sex differences are curious and so far no one has been able to explain them adequately. One theory is that female hormones give women protection from the early and severe form of the illness. Another theory relies on the established fact that men and women have different brain structures and, although they are equally intelligent overall, they have a natural disposition to excel at different things – for example, women are generally better at the use of language and expressing themselves, whereas men seem to excel in manual tasks and those requiring physical co-ordination. It may be that the critical areas of the brain which give rise to schizophrenia when they are not functioning properly are slightly different in men and women. This might explain the differences in age of onset, symptom pattern and recovery rate.

THE FAMILY TENDENCY

The general risk, for any one of us, of developing schizophrenia is 1 in 100. If, however, we have what is known as a first-degree relative with schizophrenia (a brother, sister, parent or child), that risk is increased tenfold, so that the chance becomes 1 in 10. Non-identical twins carry the same risk as a first-degree relative of 1 in 10 if their twin already has schizophrenia; identical twins, however, who share more genes than any other two human beings, have a 1 in 3 chance of developing schizophrenia if their twin has the condition. If we have a second-degree relative (such as an aunt or uncle) with schizophrenia, our chances of developing the illness are 2 in 100.

You might think that the increased familial risk is an effect of living too closely with someone who has the illness. It has been suggested, for example, that the substantially increased risk among identical as compared with non-identical twins is nothing to do with their closer genetic inheritance (in other words, the fact that they share more genes than any other two people) but due to the fact that they are emotionally closer.

This possibility has been well researched, and discounted, however. Investigators have looked at identical twins whose mothers had schizophrenia, and who were separated at birth. One was brought up by the real biological mother, the other adopted by people without any history of the condition. Most cases of schizophrenia begin in late adolescence or early adulthood, so each twin was traced 20 to 30 years later, covering the high-risk period for schizophrenia. The chance of developing schizophrenia was found to be identical in each twin. This means that we can be certain of at least one risk factor for schizophrenia: it lies in one's genes and not in one's upbringing.

If you are still curious about the 'nature–nurture' controversy – genes versus upbringing – consider these further two facts. If a child of non-schizophrenic parents is adopted at birth by someone who later turns out to develop schizophrenia, the child has no greater chance of developing schizophrenia than the normal 1 in 100. Secondly, if a child is born of a family where several members have schizophrenia, then the child's risk of developing schizophrenia is even higher than the 1 in 10 for those with a single schizophrenic first-degree relative. It approaches 1 in 5, for example, if your mother, brother and two aunts all have schizophrenia.

These two facts should convince you that developing schizophrenia has nothing to do with being brought up by someone with the condition, but has to do with the strength of the gene for schizophrenia within your family. The greater the number of close family members who have it, the greater your risk. It is as if you inherit a certain 'dose' of the gene for schizophrenia.

You may wonder how far back down the family tree you have to worry about. First-degree relatives with the condition – brother, sister, parent or child – increase your own risk by a factor of 10. Second-degree relatives with the condition – uncle, aunt, grandparent, first cousin – increase your chance by a factor of 2, raising it from 1 in 100 to 2 in 100. Having a more distant relative with the condition – such as a great aunt, second cousin and the like – conveys no appreciably greater risk than the normal 1 in 100.

Lastly, don't forget that hearing that a relative has had a 'breakdown' is no guarantee that he or she has schizophrenia. The affected person may have any of the conditions that I describe in Chapter 2. Another possibility, if the relative is a woman who has suffered a breakdown after giving birth, is that she has what psychiatrists call puerperal psychosis. This used to be regarded as a form of schizophrenia but is now considered to be a severe type of mania or depressive psychosis (*see Chapter 2*).

CHILDHOOD CHARACTER AND ADULT PERSONALITY

What Was the Sufferer Like as a Child?
Is it possible to predict the future development of schizophrenia from anything a child or young adolescent might do or say? The answer to this is no, not with any certainty. There is, however, a link between some types of childhood behaviour/some character traits and an increased risk of developing schizophrenia. The link is not strong, but is interesting for the light it throws on the nature of schizophrenia.

Most people with schizophrenia will have been entirely normal until their first breakdown. About a quarter, however, will have shown one or more of the following three abnormalities. The first is a delay in the development of language and in the development of properly co-ordinated movements. The child may have been slow to walk or talk, and even when he finally did learn, he may never have quite mastered either. Clumsiness or a speech impediment may have persisted until the child was in his teens. Secondly, parents and teachers may have noticed that attention and concentration were never his strong points. This is not the same either as exuberance or hyperactivity, which is also linked with inattention. A pre-schizophrenic child is more likely to be described as 'in a daze all the time' rather than as the hyperactive child who is 'rushing around all the time'. Thirdly, there may be a coldness, an aloofness, a difficulty in reaching the child, which has something to do with the child's inability to form emotional relationships with parents or other children.

None of these three abnormalities is invariable or even common, and many children who do not develop schizophrenia may be described in the same terms. It is often only after the diagnosis has been made that parents remember such things.

What About the Adult Personality?

In those people who develop schizophrenia in late adolescence, one cannot rightly comment on their 'personality' before the illness began because, at this stage, their personality, as the term is normally used, is not fully developed. However, in those people who develop schizophrenia in their middle twenties or later, it is certainly justifiable to remark on what their personality was like before the illness began. This is referred to by psychiatrists as the pre-morbid personality (from *morbus*, meaning illness).

In about a quarter of those who develop schizophrenia in adulthood, there will have been evidence of a *schizoid personality disorder* before any overt symptoms or signs of the illness emerge. The nature of a schizoid personality disorder was discussed in Chapter 2, because it can sometimes be mistaken for schizophrenia itself. The cluster of personality traits that make up this personality disorder, all of which need to be present in extreme degree, are:

- a liking for solitariness
- insensitivity to what others feel or think
- a pedantic use of language
- resistance to any change in the way the person thinks about the world.

In everyday language, such people may be referred to as 'cold fish', recluses or eccentrics. However, not all people described in this way develop actual schizophrenia – probably only about 1 in 10 do. And not all cases of schizophrenia beginning in adulthood have a pre-morbid schizoid personality – only about 1 in 4 do.

Possible Risk Factors

RACE AND GEOGRAPHICAL LOCATION

Schizophrenia occurs in all countries of the world at more or less the same rate. Psychiatrists have compared developing countries, such as Colombia, India and Nigeria, with others such as Great Britain, Denmark, USA and Russia and found no difference in the proportion of people with schizophrenia in the population. As one might expect, however, there are cross-cultural differences in the way in which the illness shows itself. Delusions about secret services implanting electrodes in the brain are more common in developed countries, whereas magic and voodoo are more common themes in other areas of the world. The fundamental nature of the illness, however, is the same everywhere.

Within countries there are some intriguing differences which could give us a clue to the cause of schizophrenia. However, most of these, on closer study, have turned out to be false leads.

It is known, for instance, that there are more people with schizophrenia in the deprived inner-city areas than in the countryside or affluent suburbs. At one time, this was taken as proof that there was something about urban living that caused schizophrenia. However, when the *background* of these people was examined, it became clear that it was no different from that of the average person. Proportionally, the same number had been brought up in the city as in the country. Moreover, if you looked at the whereabouts of their brothers and sisters who had not developed schizophrenia, they still tended to live in the sort of places where they and their schizophrenic brother or sister had been brought up. What had happened to the schizophrenia sufferer, therefore, was that he had gravitated towards the inner city *because* of his illness. It was not that his place of origin had caused his condition. Sufferers were found to have drifted down the social ladder, both in employment and housing status. This finding is underlined by a recent study of homeless men in London, where no less than one-third were found to have schizophrenia – in other words, 33 times the normal rate. So, far from there being something about urban living that causes schizophrenia, the truth is that schizophrenics, as a consequence of their illness, tend to drift away from their roots to the poorer parts of a city. Their failure to keep a regular job and their tendency to shun company leads them to seek out cheaper accommodation in anonymous bed-sitter land, or, worse, in hostels for the homeless.

Not all of the differences within a country can be explained in this way. There are rare pockets of high rates of schizophrenia in various parts of the world. The best investigated of these is Western Ireland, which has a rate twice or three times the average for the rest of the world, including the rest of Ireland. The reason for this is uncertain. It has been suggested that the most mentally healthy families emigrated to North America during the great famines of the 19th century, leaving behind a less mentally healthy stock. This is not a very satisfactory explanation, because most studies of immigrants have shown that schizophrenia is more common among migrants than in either the population they left behind or the indigenous population which they join. Another theory is that Irish mothers continue childbearing well into their forties, an age when the risks to the baby from complications at birth increase. One of the possible risk factors for schizophrenia (*see below*) is a history of birth complications, and this theory for the higher rate of schizophrenia in Western Ireland may have some truth in it.

Several recent studies done in England have found a higher rate of first-time episodes of schizophrenia in Afro-Caribbean people than in the general population. This increased rate is particularly pronounced in those who were born in England – in other words, second-generation Afro-Caribbeans. What this means is still the subject of research.

MILD DEGREES OF BRAIN DAMAGE

I pointed out in Chapter 2 that most types of physical damage to the brain in adulthood, if they do give rise to psychiatric symptoms, produce an entirely different psychiatric disorder from schizophrenia. If the physical damage is severe and sudden, then an acute organic illness (otherwise known as delirium) occurs (*see page 32*). If the damage affects the entire brain and builds up gradually, then a chronic organic illness (dementia) occurs (*see page 34*).

However, there are two situations in which these rules do not apply. One is during the time when the brain is still physically developing – from the foetal stage to early adolescence. The other is when the brain damage, at whatever stage of life, is not generalized, but affects only a small part of the brain. In both these situations, psychiatric symptoms may occur which are different from those of delirium or dementia, and sometimes schizophrenia may develop.

The best evidence for a link between damage to the developing brain and schizophrenia is the fact that someone who develops schizophrenia in late adolescence or adulthood will be more likely than average to have undergone complications at birth. If the mother has a prolonged labour, or the cord is twisted round the infant's neck or there is an unusual presentation of the infant, such as a breech birth, this can lead to anoxia – lack of oxygen – to the infant's brain. Part of the brain then becomes damaged. If the damage is severe, this will be obvious within weeks or months – the child will be spastic if the part of the brain which controls movements is affected, or mentally retarded if the part responsible for intellectual functions is damaged. However, if the damage is slight or is in what are known as 'silent' areas of the brain, it may go entirely unnoticed throughout childhood.

These silent areas of the brain are those which do not have a simple function such as controlling movement or representing sensation. Instead, they have an overall co-ordinating function, and the reason, it is thought, that there is such a delay before they give rise to symptoms is that it is not until adolescence that the full potential of the brain is realized. At this time, all the co-ordinating functions of the brain are needed ready to achieve the fully balanced mind of adulthood. Any minor defect which could be compensated for during childhood will now become obvious when full capacity is called for. So obstetric complications must be considered a risk factor for the development of schizophrenia. I have included it among possible risk factors because evidence as to the link is still not entirely sound, and the link, if it does exist, is anyway not a strong one: those who develop schizophrenia are only slightly more likely to have had obstetric complications than the average person, and most people who have had obstetric complications never develop schizophrenia.

Month of Birth

Another possible risk factor is being born in the winter months of the year. This might seem a strange fact, but it has been reported by several different researchers in different parts of the world. Someone who is later to develop schizophrenia tends to be born in November, December, January, February or March, rather than in other months, in the Northern Hemisphere. In Australia, it is April to September where the excess births occur, their winter months. This must mean that something that happens in winter but not other seasons has a bearing on the cause of schizophrenia. The most likely event, it is assumed, is a viral infection, which the mother in late pregnancy is more likely to contract at this time of year, and this then damages the brain of the foetus. Not all researchers have found this pattern among women whose children later developed schizophrenia, so at the moment it must be considered only as a possible risk factor.

Childhood Epilepsy

A third possible risk factor which concerns damage to the developing brain is the link between epilepsy beginning in childhood and the later development of schizophrenia. Childhood epilepsy is often due to brain damage in the area of the brain known as the temporal lobe. The brain damage may be in the form of a flaw in the proper development of this area – a cyst or a group of cells which do not divide properly and form a minute non-malignant tumour. Or it may occur in the first two years of life because the child has a series of febrile fits – seizures which occur during a very high temperature caused by influenza or other infections. Either way, the small area of brain damage disturbs the electrical stability of the brain and causes epilepsy. It is not epilepsy which is the potential risk factor, but the underlying brain damage. I have regarded it as a possible risk factor only, because the eventual psychiatric disorder, if it occurs, is not entirely typical of schizophrenia. Some psychiatrists hedge their bets and call it a 'schizophreniform psychosis'. Certainly, many of the characteristic features of schizophrenia are absent, including flattening of affect, formal thought disorder, and disordered movement (*see Chapter 1*). For these reasons, I myself am doubtful if childhood epilepsy and its underlying brain damage can correctly be considered a risk factor for true schizophrenia.

Head Injury

Finally, if brain damage of a restricted nature does occur in adulthood, for example, following a head injury, then sometimes signs of schizophrenia may occur, even years after the actual injury. As in the case of childhood epilepsy, the problem arises, however, as to whether this is true schizophrenia or not. My view is that post-traumatic schizophrenia of this nature is not the same illness as schizophrenia, which occurs out of the blue, so to speak, in late adolescence or early adulthood. For this reason, brain damage in adulthood is not a definite risk factor for true schizophrenia.

Suggested Risk Factors Which Are Now Discounted

SUPPOSEDLY BAD CHILD-REARING HABITS

It was thought at one time that parents could 'make' a child at risk of developing schizophrenia by the way they brought the child up. One psychiatrist coined the term 'schizophrenogenic mother', meaning an over-protective mother who gave conflicting messages to the child, saying, for example, 'You naughty boy,' but smiling at the same time. The child, it was claimed, would grow up never knowing whether people were cross or pleased with him. Other psychiatrists thought they could identify a pattern of abnormal family communication which could leave the child damaged for life in his or her ability to express coherent thoughts or understand the real meaning of what others were saying.

There is virtually no evidence whatsoever that faulty upbringing, unresolved family tensions or having domineering parents places a child at risk of developing schizophrenia.

STRESS

There is little or no evidence either that stress or emotional upheavals in adulthood can render someone more liable than otherwise to develop schizophrenia. This means that whatever bad things might happen to you in your life – bereavement, extreme disappointment, stress at work or in personal relationships – this in itself will not cause you to develop schizophrenia. It may make you anxious, depressed or even paranoid, but not schizophrenic. In other words, any of the neuroses can be caused by psychological factors, so can either of the affective psychoses, and even paranoia if there is a pre-existing personality disorder. Schizophrenia, however, appears to be immune from such life events.

There are a large number of research studies in support of the view that psychological factors are unimportant in causing schizophrenia. Many men, in battle, for example, break down eventually from a combination of extreme exhaustion, fear and relentless bombardment; but they develop panic, depression or hysteria, not schizophrenia. The aftermath of natural disasters, such as hurricanes or earthquakes, also produces many psychiatric casualties, but they take the form of neuroses, not schizophrenia.

DIETARY PATTERNS

Many people believe that an unhealthy diet, vitamin deficiency or allergy to certain foodstuffs makes someone at risk of developing schizophrenia. I do not want to dismiss any of these theories out of hand because, as schizophrenia is a mysterious disease and as we do not know everything about the good and bad effects of certain diets, it would be foolish to take a black-and-white view of the matter. All I would say is that any dietary theory of schizophrenia has to fit the few facts about the condition that we know.

In the first place, people's dietary habits differ widely, according to culture and inclination, and yet there is no culture and no country in the world where schizophrenia does not occur. Certainly in my experience of over 1,000 people with schizophrenia, I have never seen anyone who was brought up on a particularly unusual diet.

Secondly, although vitamin deficiencies do occur in families who cannot afford adequate diets, schizophrenia knows no class difference. It is not a disease of the under-privileged, and cannot be linked with inadequate diet.

Finally, people who do suffer from certain specific food allergies — coeliac disease, for example, in which the intestine becomes inflamed and cannot absorb an essential ingredient of wheat — are no more liable to develop schizophrenia than anyone else. For all these reasons, I believe that dietary theories of schizophrenia are incorrect.

5

WHAT CAUSES SCHIZOPHRENIA?

The ultimate cause of schizophrenia is a mystery. It is one of the riddles of mankind. Well, you might think, what is the point of including this chapter in the book? There are three reasons. First, it is probably the most common question that I am asked about schizophrenia, by both relatives and people with schizophrenia, and so you should know the current theories. Secondly, it is not a complete mystery, because we can now say with some certainty what does *not* cause schizophrenia. This in itself is helpful because some of the causes suggested in the past – particular forms of child-rearing, for example – laid blame on the parents, which is now seen as both incorrect and harmful. Thirdly, in recent years some of the mystery has been unravelled, at least in the area of what is happening in the mind and the brain of the sufferer.

What Is Meant by 'Cause'?

In the last chapter, we considered the factors that make someone at greater risk than average of developing schizophrenia. None of these, however, even the most definite, can be considered a cause of schizophrenia because none of them is invariably found in the background of someone with schizophrenia. Moreover, the cause of an altered psychological state, such as schizophrenia, cannot be completely reduced to a physical abnormality. Even if an abnormal gene were to be found on one of the chromosomes, and some researchers have claimed to have found just this – on chromosome 5 – one still has to account for the intervening stages whereby an abnormal gene or some other ultimate cause produces (possibly) an abnormal chemical which then alters brain function which in turn alters psychological functions.

In considering the cause of schizophrenia, therefore, we have to take into account at least four levels:

1. the psychological level
2. the brain functional level
3. the chemical level
4. the ultimate level.

PSYCHOLOGICAL CAUSE

By 'psychological cause' I do not mean untoward events in our social or emotional lives. As I discussed in Chapter 4, these are not important in bringing about a schizophrenic illness. I am referring instead to the psychological functions of the mind – particularly perception, language, thinking and control of movement. What happens to these functions in order to produce the characteristic symptoms and signs of schizophrenia?

In a normal person, each of these main functions has several components. In the case of language, for example, there is a system which generates speech sounds, another which perceives the speech sounds of others, another which provides the meaning of words, and yet another which assesses the value of an utterance for purposes of social communication. In the case of perception, there is a system which specializes in the detection of detail – say the colour of someone's eyes – another which computes the three-dimensional qualities of the world – allowing, for example, a fielder in cricket to place himself ready for a catch, or anyone to size up the general physiognomy of a face. In a normal person, the various components within a main function are in balance and complement one another, thus allowing us to carry out efficiently any task in hand. To take the example of perception, if we look at a face, we can either concentrate on the colour of the eyes, or try and assess the personality of its owner. We do the former by calling up the system which specializes in detail, the latter by taking a more global approach – a combined evaluation, perhaps, of shape of jaw, size of eyes, and hairstyle – a procedure which requires the computation of the spatial layout of these features in a three-dimensional matrix. Some normal people may be more drawn to one aspect of a face than others. Men, for example, are notoriously bad at remembering eye colour, even that of their wives. But a normal person *can* shift from one aspect to another when required to, using for this purpose first one perceptual system, then another.

The essence of the psychological problem in schizophrenia is that the various components within each main function are *not in balance* and *no longer complement* one another. Moreover, within each main function there is a *shift towards the regular reliance on one or some of the components at the expense of another or others*. To continue the example of face perception, there is a shift towards the accentuation of detail at the expense of appreciating the overall configuration of things. This explains the experience of Denise (*page 10*), for whom colours were vivid but faces distorted, or that of Stella (*page 11*), for whom people looked like 'ghosts ... statues ... monuments ... dead or cremated'. The point about this shift in someone with schizophrenia is that, unlike a normal person, he or she cannot move smoothly from one component to another; it is as if schizophrenics are stuck with the one that is exaggerated.

Most of the characteristic symptoms and signs of schizophrenia can be explained in a comparable way, with reference to patterns of exaggerated and diminished strength of components within each major mental function. This is why the word schizophrenia is so apt – a splitting of the mind, with one component, previously camouflaged by another, now being shown in stark relief.

Consider the peculiar use of language in the extract of the writings of one of Eugen Bleuler's patients (*page 7*), or the man who was fascinated by chimneys (*page 14*). Technically referred to as formal thought disorder, the most striking feature is the lack of concern for the communication value of language. The component of language and thought which monitors whether what we say will be understood by our listener or reader is clearly virtually defunct here. On the other hand, there is an abundance of newly invented words or new definitions of real words and objects. One can consider this as evidence that the component of language which provides meanings of words has gone berserk, and is grossly overactive, in contrast with the underactivity of the component that monitors a word's social value.

The disordered expressions of emotion in face or voice, referred to as flattening or inappropriate affect (*page 20*), are also a consequence, respectively, of underactivity in the general control of facial movement and vocal inflection, and occasional bursts of over-activity in a separate system responsible for the expression of happiness – hence uncontrolled and empty giggling, for example.

There are psychological explanations along these lines for the voices which many people with schizophrenia hear, and for the characteristic delusions that they are under someone else's control. (The explanations are, however, more complicated than for general perceptual disorder, formal thought disorder and blunted and inappropriate effect. The interested reader is advised to turn to my books *The Right Cerebral Hemisphere and Psychiatric Disorders* [Oxford University Press, 1990] or *Two Worlds, Two Minds, Two Hemispheres* [Oxford University Press, 1996] for a suggested explanation of these.)

So, at the first level, at least, the psychological cause of the signs and symptoms of schizophrenia is not so mysterious. They come about chiefly though a shift in emphasis from one set of component systems within a major mental function – such as perception, language or movement control – to another set within the same major mental function. What this shift could itself be caused by is considered next.

BRAIN FUNCTIONAL DISTURBANCE

Each of the mental functions (including their components, mentioned above) has a specific site within the brain (*see Figures on page 117*). Of the components of language mentioned, for example, the system generating speech is situated in the lower front section of the left hemisphere (left inferior frontal lobe); that responsible for the perception of speech lies in the upper lateral section of the left hemisphere (left superior temporal lobe). Meanings of words are represented over a large area of the lateral section of the left hemisphere (chiefly the left temporal and parietal lobes). The social and communication value of language is provided by large areas of the right hemisphere (right frontal, temporal and parietal lobes). The two components of perception mentioned, the analysis of detail and the computation of three-dimensional space, are situated respectively in the left hind section of the brain (left parietal, temporal and occipital lobes) and the right hind section of the brain (right parietal, temporal and occipital lobes).

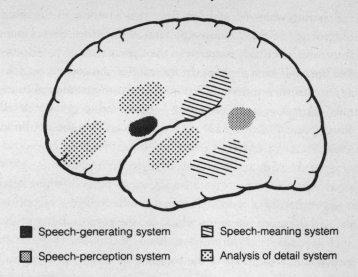

- ■ Speech-generating system
- ▨ Speech-perception system
- ▤ Speech-meaning system
- ⊡ Analysis of detail system

The left hemisphere of the brain, showing the areas that generate, perceive, and define the meaning of speech, and that control analysis of detail

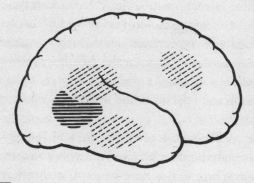

- ▨ Social and communication value of language system
- ▤ Computation of three-dimensional space system

The right hemisphere of the brain, showing the areas that process the communication value of language and compute three-dimensional space

Knowing which mental functions reside where in the brain is important so that a known pattern of *disordered mental functioning* can be quickly mapped to the site or sites of its responsible *disturbed brain function*. In the case of schizophrenia, taking the disordered pattern within the two major mental functions — language and perception — discussed in greater detail above (*pages 114 and 115*), it seems clear that the common denominator in terms of disturbed brain function has something to do with an incompetent right hemisphere. It is the social value of language and the ability to perceive the spatial configuration of objects that are most affected in schizophrenia, and these are functions which are the responsibility of the right hemisphere. On the other hand, the ability to generate speech and to understand the meaning of words, to recognize others' speech, and to perceive details in the environment are intact or even enhanced, and it is these functions which are the special province of the left hemisphere. We are drawn to the conclusion, therefore, that the pattern of exaggeration versus decline of the mental functions in schizophrenia exactly parallels a pattern of exaggeration versus decline of the left and right hemispheres respectively. This situation we can refer to as *functional imbalance* between the two hemispheres, where one, the left, is temporarily overactive relative to its own normal condition and relative to the usual level of activity of the right.

All the psychological problems in schizophrenia (which themselves underlie the characteristic symptoms and signs of the condition) can, in my view, be explained in terms of this shift towards one hemisphere (the left) taking on more of the responsibility for the mental life of a person than before, and the right giving up a proportional amount. (The fundamental differences between the two hemispheres of the brain has only come to light in the last 40 years. This surprising gap in human knowledge has, in my view, contributed to the delay in understanding schizophrenia. For further reading about the hemispheres, especially the right, which has been particularly neglected, I would refer you again to *The Right Cerebral Hemisphere and Psychiatric Disorders* [OUP, 1990].)

So far, I have attempted to explain how the symptoms and signs of schizophrenia arise out of disordered mental functions and then how these disordered mental functions have their basis in disturbed brain functions. The next question is how this functional imbalance, the shift between hemispheric parity to one of left-hemisphere dominance, comes about. The next section, on chemical imbalance, provides one answer.

CHEMICAL IMBALANCE

There are about two dozen substances, and more are discovered every year, which act as chemical messengers in the brain. Each of the millions of nerve cells in the brain is entirely separate from the others. When one of them is stimulated, a minute electrical current is generated which passes from one end of the cell to the other. When it reaches the other end, it does not jump to the next cell but instead causes the release of a small amount of chemical which then flows to the next cell, generating an electrical current in that cell, and so on. Different types of cells release different chemicals. Not all of these chemicals stimulate their neighbours; some inhibit the cell they flow to. If the supply of one of these chemicals dries up or if it is overproduced or if the target cells become supersensitive to it, then a whole series of things can happen, depending on what part of the brain is affected, what the chemical does and whether it is in excess or in limited supply.

Parkinson's disease is a relatively simple example of chemical imbalance. This is a condition in which movements become slower and more laborious until finally the sufferer cannot move at all. It is caused by the gradual death, for unknown reasons, of a collection of cells in the lower part of the brain which normally supply the rest of the brain with one of the main neurotransmitters – dopamine. As the supply of dopamine to the part of the brain responsible for initiating movements dries up, so does the sufferer's ability to start movements or change to a different movement. At the same time, the supply of another neurotransmitter – acetyl choline – increases in compensation and this causes involuntary movements such as tremor. Parkinson's disease is treated most effectively by a drug called L-dopa, which is broken down in the body to dopamine and thus replenishes the supply. The other symptoms, caused by too much acetyl choline, can be cured by giving the patient another drug which partially blocks the effect of acetyl choline. The chemical imbalance is thus restored and the sufferer returns to normal.

Many psychiatrists believe that schizophrenia is caused by a similar imbalance involving dopamine, except that in the case of schizophrenia they claim that the dopamine is in excess of what it should be and not the other way round. If this is true, from what we know of Parkinson's disease one would expect the symptoms of schizophrenia to be those of intense restlessness and overactivity, something which is true of mania but not schizophrenia. Proponents of this theory, however, point out that dopamine is not found in all parts of the brain, and there is one study showing that it is only in excess in the left hemisphere. A selective, localized excess of dopamine might therefore account for the particular pattern of psychological and brain functional disturbance seen in schizophrenia.

The main reason for taking the dopamine theory of schizophrenia seriously is that all the drugs which are effective in curing the signs of schizophrenia are dopamine-blockers. It would be strange, therefore, if excessive dopamine did not have something to do with schizophrenia.

An excess or reduction in several of the other known neu-rotransmitters has also been blamed as the cause of schizo-phrenia. One of these — 5 hydroxytrypt-amine, or 5HT — has a chemical formula almost identical to a street drug called dimethyltryptamine, or DMT, taken for its hallucinogenic properties. It was thought by some psychiatrists that if people with schizophrenia lacked the enzyme to manufacture this correctly in the body they might produce DMT — the hallu-cinogenic — rather than 5HT — the harmless neurotransmitter. In fact, the sort of hallucinations produced by the drug DMT and others of this group (such as LSD and mescaline) are quite unlike those experienced by people with schizophrenia, nor do they give rise to the other characteristic signs, such as changes in the expression of speech, emotions and movement.

Of all the chemical theories of schizophrenia, therefore, the dopamine theory is by far the best because it explains why antischizophrenic drugs are effective. Many psychiatrists, how-ever, myself included, find it unsatisfactory because it does not account for the imbalance between different components of a main mental function nor for the imbalance between different hemispheres, with the exception of the one study mentioned above.

Chemical imbalance, however, at least provides a plausible explanation for how the ultimate cause of schizophrenia could modify brain function, thereby producing the particular psy-chological disorder which I believe underlies the symptoms and signs of the condition.

We now turn to theories about the ultimate cause of the condition.

CONCLUSION

This is the real riddle of schizophrenia. The most certain facts concern what does *not* cause it rather than what *does*.

It is not caused, for example, by improper child-rearing, nor by marital discord or divorce in the parents. It is not caused either by lack of vitamins or other dietary insufficiencies.

It may be caused by an abnormal gene, but the precise location of this is still under investigation. In some people, however, it may have nothing to do with their genetic make-up but be a delayed consequence of definite brain damage at or around the time of birth. This may appear confusing, as in the section on brain functional disturbances (above) I said that the hemispheric imbalance was not based on definite brain damage. The theory of hemisphere imbalance, however, assumes that the nerve cells function differently in this situation, passing messages *perversely* rather than being obliterated in their true function by structural damage. It assumes that a small area of structural damage, during development, in one part of the brain has a *distant* effect on the rest of the apparently normal brain, by virtue of the fact that it holds some co-ordinating role in normal people. In this sense, true structural damage in a small critical area might affect the function of the whole brain by acting at a distance, and thereby be an ultimate cause of schizophrenia.

6

HOW SCHIZOPHRENIA IS TREATED

Over the last century a great diversity of treatments have been used in the treatment of schizophrenia, with markedly varying degrees of success. By far the most successful of these has been a class of drugs known as *neuroleptics*. In this chapter I shall discuss the various treatments used by psychiatrists, including:

- drug treatment with neuroleptics
- biological treatments other than drugs, notably electro-convulsive therapy (ECT)
- psychological treatments, including psychotherapy, family therapy, behaviour therapy and self-control (cognitive therapy)
- social treatments, including occupational therapy while in hospital and recommendation for a change in living style when outside hospital.

I shall also be looking in this chapter at sources of profession-al help, and at who, in addition to the consultant psychiatrist, is involved in the treatment of the acute stage of schizophrenia and in rehabilitation programmes over the long term. The issue of alternative therapies (dietary change and megavitamin therapy) is also considered. Lastly, the questions of where treatment is to be obtained and where it is to be carried out are explored.

Drug Treatments

Many people with schizophrenia, and their relatives as well, dislike the idea of drug treatments for the illness. In this section I shall attempt to resolve many of the common questions about drug treatments. These include:

- What are the drugs?
- Tablets or injection?
- The correct dosage?
- What are the side-effects?
- How do the drugs work?
- What are the advantages of one drug over another?
- For how long should they be taken?
- Must they be taken?
- Are there alternative (non-neuroleptic) drugs?

CHLORPROMAZINE

The turning point in the treatment of schizophrenia came in 1952 when two French psychiatrists, Jean Delay and Paul Deniker, reported the successful use of a drug called chlorpromazine. Like most effective treatments in medicine, it was a chance discovery.

Chlorpromazine is one of a family of drugs known as phenothiazines which had been manufactured in the United States years before and which were known to have a *large* number of different actions (hence its trade name in Britain – Largactil). Other members of this drug family had been used to cure, for example, worms in animals, to sterilize the bladder before operations, to reduce sneezing in hay fever and to make anaesthetics more powerful.

Chlorpromazine was noticed to have a calming effect and it was for this reason that it was tried on schizophrenics. Delay and Deniker noticed that its calming effect was different from that of tranquillizers such as barbiturates (which were the standard treatment for anxiety at that time, before diazepam [Valium] was manufactured). Delay and Deniker called chlorpromazine a *neuroleptic* because it had a much finer action on the nervous system than the blunderbuss effect of tranquillizers – *leptos* in Greek means 'comb', and *neuro* means 'nerves'.

At first, psychiatrists around the world were sceptical of the claims made for chlorpromazine. Their scepticism was understandable: over the previous 50 years there had been hundreds of suggested remedies, all of which had turned out to be ineffective, if not downright harmful. These included, for example, insulin coma – causing coma by injecting insulin with the aim of reducing the brain's sugar level to a critical degree; leucotomy – surgical division of the brain's nerve fibres in a 'silent' area in the front of the brain; and electroconvulsive therapy (ECT) – a course of electric shocks to the brain.

It soon became clear that chlorpromazine was no passing fad, but an astonishingly effective drug. People with schizophrenia who had been in the long-stay wards of mental hospitals for decades recovered in weeks, and could be discharged virtually free of all signs of the illness. Before the 1950s, about two in three people with schizophrenia had to remain in hospital for the rest of their lives. Today, only about 1 in 20 needs continuous hospital care.

OTHER NEUROLEPTICS
Since chlorpromazine appeared, other drugs for the treatment

of schizophrenia have been introduced. Some of them are from the same family as chlorpromazine (the phenothiazine family) and some are not, but they are all neuroleptics. In general, they all have the same beneficial effects as chlorpromazine, but they differ in the extent to which an individual will respond to each, and in the side-effects they may produce. Commonly prescribed neuroleptics are listed in Table 1. Most people with schizophrenia will be taking one of these drugs. The remainder may be prescribed one of the less commonly used neuroleptics (*see Table 2*). In the last few years two novel neuroleptics have been introduced – clozapine (Clozaril) and risperidone (Risperdal). These are for sufferers who have not responded to the conventional neuroleptics. They are listed in Table 2.

TABLETS OR INJECTION?

Some of the drugs are taken by mouth – oral preparations – and some are given by injection – intramuscular preparations. The latter are of two types – short-acting, which last as long as the oral preparations (about a day); and long-acting, which last about three to four weeks. These long-acting preparations contain the drug in an oily fluid which seeps out of the muscles of the buttocks over the month and gives a steady level of the drug in the bloodstream. The oral and short-acting intramuscular drugs are for the acute stage of the illness; the long-acting ones are intended to prevent a recurrence when the acute stage is over.

Table 1: Commonly used neuroleptics for the treatment of schizophrenia

Official name (the chemical compound)	Proprietary name (UK) (given by the company that makes the drug)	Dose (usual daily dose)	Route (how they are taken)
Family 1			
chlorpromazine	Largactil	400–800 mg daily	orally (by mouth)
trifluoperazine	Stelazine	10–20 mg daily	orally
thioridazine	Melleril	400–800 mg daily	orally
fluphenazine	Modecate	25–37.5 mg monthly	intramuscularly (injection into muscle)
Family 2			
haloperidol	Dozic, Fortunan Haldol, Serenace	5–20 mg daily 100–200 mg monthly	orally intramuscularly
Family 3			
flupenthixol	Depixol	40 mg every 3 weeks	intramuscularly
zuclopenthixol	Clopixol	200 mg every 3 weeks or 30–60 mg daily	intramuscularly orally
Family 4			
pimozide	Orap	4–8 mg daily	orally
Family 5			
sulpiride	Dolmatil	400–800 mg daily	orally

Most people with schizophrenia will be prescribed one of the drugs shown in Table 1. If you cannot find the name of the drug you wish to check, turn to Table 2 (page 128), which shows those drugs prescribed for the remaining sufferers.

Each drug has two or more names. It always has one and only one official name, by which it is known the world over. This is the name of the chemical compound. Then it has one or more proprietary, brand or trade names, given by the company or companies that make the drug. Each drug company who makes it calls it by their own brand name. So, in Great Britain, May and Baker are the main company producing chlorpromazine, and they call it Largactil. In the United States, the company which produces it calls it Thorazine. Drugs that are off-patent, which include chlorpromazine, may have several different trade names in the same country. Haloperidol, for instance, has four trade names in Britain alone — Dozic, Fortunan, Haldol and Serenace. It is better to learn the official name if you can, because if you go abroad and need a repeat prescription doctors there will probably never have heard of the British name. Unfortunately, the official name is usually harder to remember.

Table 2: Less commonly used neuroleptics for the treatment of schizophrenia

Official name	Proprietary name (UK)	Dose	Route
chlorprothixene	Taractan	45–150 mg daily	orally (by mouth)
droperidol	Droleptan	10–40 mg daily	intramuscularly (injection into muscle)
fluspirilene	Redeptin	2–8 mg weekly	intramuscularly
perphenazine	Fentazin	12–24 mg daily	orally
pipothiazine	Piportil	50–100 mg weekly	intramuscularly
Novel neuroleptics:			
clozapine	Clozaril	200–600 mg daily	orally
risperidone	Risperdal	6–10 mg daily	orally

Most people with schizophrenia will be prescribed one of the drugs shown in Table 1. The remainder may be prescribed one of these less commonly used neuroleptics listed in Table 2. A few sufferers may be prescribed a non-neuroleptic, in other words a drug that is not specifically intended for use in the treatment of schizophrenia (see Alternative Drugs, page 140).

Some people hate injections and prefer to take tablets even for prevention. The oral and long-acting intramuscular preparations are equally effective in preventing a recurrence, but because even the most intelligent and conscientious people are unreliable when it comes to remembering to take tablets, I usually advise my patients to have injections. Sufferers have to remember only to turn up regularly at the hospital outpatients' clinic or at their general practitioner – every three weeks for some preparations, every four weeks for others. Most hospitals in Britain run what is called a depot clinic for this purpose. Here the patient does not have to wait around to see the psychiatrist but can just contact the nurse in charge and be in and out in under half an hour. Sometimes these clinics function outside working hours. Some hospitals have community psychiatric nurses who will make a home visit to give the injection.

WHAT DOSE?

Each drug has a different effective, or therapeutic, dose range. This does not mean that one is stronger than another. If I change a patient's prescription from, say, trifluoperazine (Stelazine) to chlorpromazine (Largactil), the patient often thinks he or she is being given a stronger drug, because the effective dose of the former is only 10–20 mg a day whereas the equivalent in chlorpromazine is 400–800 mg daily.

The dose is absolutely crucial. Each drug has a range – the therapeutic dose – at which it works. Too little and it won't work, too much and it can often prove counter-productive. There is a *lower limit* below which the drug does not work. One would not take a quarter of an aspirin, for example, for a raging headache. Most of us know that the effective dose of aspirin to relieve an adult headache is two to three 300 mg tablets every four hours, depending on body weight.

There is also an *upper limit* for each drug. The exact level varies from person to person, because there are individual variations in the speed of absorption, metabolism and excretion. The majority of people, however, rarely need more than twice the lower limit. This rule may be broken in the early stage of an acute episode because the sufferer may be so disturbed that there is a considerable chance that he will seriously hurt himself or someone else. In such circumstances the higher dose of drug is being used purely for its tranquillizing properties. Most acute schizophrenic episodes will clear up within four to six weeks with adequate medication, and there is rarely any need to keep up high doses after the first month. Quite often the illness has been untreated for months or even years before the sufferer first comes to the attention of a psychiatrist (or first agrees to). This is not at all uncommon. In such cases the length of time before the symptoms recede may be much longer – three to six months even. Everyone concerned should be patient in such circumstances, if possible, because increasing the dose will not speed up the process of improvement, and may hinder it.

There is a tendency among some psychiatrists to over-prescribe – to give several antischizophrenic drugs instead of one, or to give too high a dose of any one. This is usually harmful because the variety and the severity of *side-effects* increase with dose, whereas going above the therapeutic range does not increase the *beneficial effects*. In fact, there may be a decrease in effectiveness at high doses, although this is not proven. There is no need, moreover, to take more than one preparation.

WHAT ARE THE SIDE-EFFECTS?

Unfortunately, like all good drugs, those used for treating schizophrenia have side-effects. Virtually all drugs that have any good effect also have side-effects. You should know what these are because most of them are preventable, either by altering the dose, changing to another preparation or by taking another type of drug in addition to the antischizophrenic drug.

I have listed the most common side-effects in Table 3 under three headings – disturbances of movement, general mental symptoms and bodily symptoms.

Table 3: Side-effects of antischizophrenic drugs

Side-effect	Technical name	Treatment
Disturbance in movement		
Stiffness in neck and face with involuntary twitching	Dystonia	Procyclidine 10–20 mg daily or orphenadrine 100–200 mg daily
Slowing up of movement	Parkinsonian symptoms	Reduce antischizophrenic drugs or give procyclidine or orphenadrine in same doses as above
Restlessness or inner sense of unease or anxiety	Akathisia	Procyclidine or orphenadrine, as above
Involuntary chewing, grimacing and tongue-rolling movements with rocking of the body	Tardive dyskinesia	Stop all antischizophrenic drugs if at all possible and wait for improvement
General mental symptoms		
General dulling of senses	Drowsiness, apathy, flatness	Reduce medication to absolute minimum or, failing that, try another drug
Bodily symptoms		
Increase in weight	Weight gain	Reduce medication to minimum or, failing that, try another drug
Increased vulnerability to sunburn	Skin photosensitivity	Reduce medication to minimum or, failing that, try another drug
Low blood-pressure on standing up quickly, producing feelings of faintness	Postural hypotension	Reduce medication to minimum or, failing that, try another drug

The most common, by far, are disturbances of movement. Although their technical names are rather daunting, the actual symptoms are not difficult to recognize, either by sufferers themselves or by a relative or psychiatrist. These side-effects are the cause of much unnecessary misery and lead many people with schizophrenia to refuse medication, with the almost inevitable result that their illness returns or worsens. Knowing what the side-effects are and how to treat them is, therefore, a crucial part of good treatment. It is claimed that the novel neuroleptics (clozapine, risperidone) do not have such marked movement side-effects. It is too early in their use to be sure of this, however.

Stiff Neck and Facial Twitches

In altered muscle tone, known as dystonia, the muscle feels stiff and may twist involuntarily. The muscles most affected are those of the face, neck and eyes. The neck muscles feel as if they are moving against one's will – they feel awkward – and this is accompanied by a general feeling of unpleasantness. The face may feel stiff and peculiar. The eyes may roll up on their own or the eyelids may twitch. All this occurs, if it does happen, after the very first few doses of an antischizophrenic drug. It nearly always wears off and rarely recurs even if higher doses are given later. It is completely curable with two tablets (or by injection if the stiffness and twitching are very acute and distressing) of another family of drugs known as anticholinergics.

When I talked about Parkinson's disease (*see Chapter 5*), I said that some of the symptoms were caused by too little dopamine and others by a compensatory increase of a neurotransmitter substance called acetylcholine. As the antischizophrenic drugs block the production of dopamine, their action leads to an excess of acetylcholine in the body. This excess acetylcholine causes the dystonia – the stiffness and twitching. Procyclidine or orphenadrine redress the balance. These 'balancing' drugs are therefore known as anticholinergics. If symptoms persist, the daily dose of procyclidine is 10–20 mg daily, or of orphenadrine 100–200 mg daily. Although people taking antischizophrenic drugs may need one or other of these at the beginning, within a month or two they themselves can begin to tail off the dose and just keep a small supply if they feel a temporary recurrence of symptoms. In the day or two after an injection of one of the long-acting preparations there is sometimes a slight peak of the level of the drug in the bloodstream; sufferers may feel better if they take two tablets of procyclidine or orphenadrine only on these days.

Slowing Up

The drugs may cause a sense of slowing up of movement, known as Parkinsonian symptoms. The side-effects are described as 'Parkinsonian' for their similarity to the signs of Parkinson's disease. The drugs do not cause this disease, however. This sense of slowing up may creep up gradually over a period of weeks and may not be given the attention it deserves either by psychiatrists or relatives. It is usually a sign that the dose of antischizophrenic drugs is too high; if it occurs at low to moderate doses, however, it is almost completely removed by the 'balancing' anticholinergic drugs described above, such as procyclidine or orphenadrine at the same doses as for the treatment of dystonia.

Restlessness

One of the side-effects of antischizophrenic drugs is a condition known as akathisia, in which the sufferer feels a strong sense of restlessness. Sufferers may not be able to sit still for even short periods of time, or may just feel an inner unease as if they do not know quite what to do with themselves. It is a sort of anxiety and agitation mixed with a desire to get up and move. It is frequently unrecognized by psychiatrists and by relatives, or may be taken by the psychiatrist as a sign of continuing psychosis and, sadly, treated with an increase in antischizophrenic drugs. However, like the side-effects of dystonia and Parkinsonian symptoms, this restlessness is completely eliminated if the drugs are stopped, much improved if the dose is reduced, tends to get better with time even if the dose of antischizophrenic drugs remains the same, and is helped enormously by procyclidine or orphenadrine in the same doses as for the side-effects described above (*see also Table 3*).

Chewing, Grimacing and Rocking

These side-effects are all part of tardive dyskinesia, which means disordered movements (dyskinesia) that are late to develop (tardive). Tardive dyskinesia is a serious side-effect of the antischizophrenic drugs because it does not clear up immediately the drugs are stopped, and there is no antidote as there is for the other disorders of movement. It consists of movements of the tongue, lips and jaw over which the sufferer has no control. Sometimes the fingers twitch and sometimes the stomach and hips gyrate. The mouth movements make it look as if sufferers are chewing or grimacing, or playing with their tongue and, surprisingly, they seem unconcerned by them. The condition is worse in older sufferers, and is rare before the age of 50. The condition is a particular nuisance because it gets even worse, paradoxically, immediately after the antischizophrenic drugs are stopped or reduced. However, it tends to improve if the drugs are stopped for a long time, and may completely disappear if the drugs can be dispensed with altogether.

Drowsiness, Apathy, Flatness

The movement disorders I have described above are less of a problem than they sound, as they are mostly treatable. The only really troublesome one is tardive dyskinesia, and this is more distressing to the relatives, as the sufferer feels no discomfort. The others can be sorted out by carefully juggling with medication. The side-effect that I receive most complaints about is a general feeling of reduced alertness. It is difficult to find the right word for it because patients describe it in different terms.

It is not really drowsiness – the sort of feeling you might experience if you were tired or if you had taken a sleeping pill the night before. The whole point about antischizophrenic drugs is that they are not simple tranquillizers like diazepam (Valium), not at the correct doses at any rate (recommended in Tables 1 and 2). This was the striking feature of them from the very beginning, when French psychiatrists Delay and Deniker first tried them out. Nor is it simply a general apathy, although this is part of what the sufferer complains of. The effect has more to do with a slight dulling of the senses, as if the world is not as sharp as it used to be and the mind not so acute.

Some patients on the drugs never mention it at all; others complain bitterly about it, preferring to stop the drugs and risk recurrence (which almost inevitably occurs) rather than feel as they do. I take their complaint very seriously because there is no point going through life if the world seems dull and uninteresting all the time. I should say that sometimes the complaint is a feature of schizophrenia itself – the blunting of emotional responses which I discussed in Chapter 1 – rather than a side-effect of the drug used in treatment. It is therefore important to tease out what is due to the illness and what to its treatment. I have found that the newer antischizophrenic drugs are less likely to cause this side-effect, and if the current drug cannot be reduced any further I try zuclopenthixol or sulpiride (*see Table 1*), often with satisfactory results.

Weight Gain, Light and Sun Sensitivity, Low Blood-pressure

These three bodily symptoms, particularly weight gain, are a nuisance. Skin photosensitivity (a heightened susceptibility to sunburn) is the least troublesome, but sufferers should be aware of it if they live in, or intend travelling to, hot countries. Postural hypotension (a tendency for the blood-pressure to drop and cause a sense of faintness on standing up quickly) is not common, but sufferers and relatives should also know about it.

Weight gain is very variable. Some patients put on several stone on low doses, some put on nothing on large doses. Some drugs are said by the manufacturers to cause less weight gain than others, but in my view it all depends on the individual. If weight gain is a problem I prescribe an alternative drug.

HOW DO THE DRUGS WORK?

All that is known about this is that all antischizophrenic drugs interfere with the neurotransmitter chemical, dopamine. How this cures the symptoms is not at all clear. I have mentioned the role of dopamine in the context of schizophrenia in Chapter 5.

WHAT ARE THE ADVANTAGES OF ONE DRUG OVER ANOTHER?

There is little to choose between the antischizophrenic drugs from the point of view of their effectiveness, provided that the dose is right for each. If someone does not respond within the expected period, however – three to six weeks for acute episodes caught at an early stage; three to six months for chronic illnesses that have been untreated for months or years – then I try changing to another family of drugs.

The most obvious advantages of one drug over another are the absence of side-effects. All these drugs have the same range of side-effects that I have mentioned, but there is so much individual variation that simply changing from one to another, at the correct dose, even within the same family of drugs, can abolish the side-effect or at least reduce it substantially.

Both psychiatrists and patients have prejudices about which is best, for reasons that may not be entirely rational. A patient may have had a bad side-effect from one drug in the past, and even though this was because it was given at too high a dose he or she may refuse to take it again, even at a lower dose. Psychiatrists may have strong views about one or other because they had a chance string of successes with one drug and a chance string of failures with another.

If you refer back to the section entitled Tablets or Injection? you will see that tablets are intended for the acute stage of the illness and long-acting intramuscular injections for the prevention of a recurrence of the illness once the acute stage has passed. Injections are easier to remember and, perhaps, more convenient, but this advantage does not particularly matter if the sufferer states a clear preference for tablets and is confident about remembering to take them.

FOR HOW LONG SHOULD THEY BE TAKEN?

This is the most difficult question I am asked. My own experience and that of all the research studies carried out is that a recurrence of the illness is *almost inevitable* after stopping the drugs, *if there have been at least two closely separated episodes of definite schizophrenia which have responded to the drugs*. It is a difficult question to be asked because although what I have just said may be true, it is a bitter disappointment to someone to be told this. It may be so much of a blow that they refuse treatment even in the short-term. If I say, 'Well, we'll review it in a year or two,' then they may comply over this period, but when they ask again and I say, 'Well, just a little longer,' then my credibility falls and the sufferer may be desperately disappointed.

I used to be less adamant about the near inevitability of the recurrence of the illness, partly because the research evidence about inevitable relapse was less certain 10 years ago, and partly because some psychiatrists at that time were recommending 'drug holidays', in the belief that some sufferers benefited from a complete rest from medication. These days research shows that relapse is more likely if medication is discontinued. If sufferers are determined to stop their medication there is, of course, nothing I can do, unless they have been involuntarily detained on a legal section (*see Chapter* 7) which compels them to take it. You can plead and cajole, that is all. Like many things in life only personal experience can teach you to take one course or other. Many sufferers, I have found, learn from bitter experience that medication, even with side-effects, is preferable to continual hospital admissions.

You may have noted that I qualified my statement at the beginning of this section with four provisos: (1) there should have been at least two separate episodes; (2) they should have been close together in time; (3) they should have been definite schizophrenia; and (4) they should have responded to the drugs.

Quite often someone is put on antischizophrenic drugs after one breakdown and then discharged back to his or her general practitioner without further review. The breakdown itself may have been vague in nature: it may not have been definite schizophrenia. This, therefore, is bad practice. A substantial minority of people who have had one definite schizophrenic illness – about 1 in 5 – will never have another one, even on no medication. No one should commit others to a lifetime of medication if they will not benefit from it. However, after two episodes the chance of recurrence without medication increases enormously, especially if the episodes follow one another in rapid succession. If the illness did not respond to the drugs in the first place there is no point, of course, in continuing them.

MUST THEY BE TAKEN?

Sufferers sometimes reject drugs, and this is an important issue as it involves more than just fear and dislike of side-effects. There are several reasons for it, and these differ from one person to another.

The most common reason is a belief that schizophrenia is not an illness, not something imposed from outside, but part of the natural progression of one's life. Many people with schizophrenia on recovery from one episode will admit that they had a breakdown and that their ideas were temporarily crazy, but refuse to accept that it was an illness. They attribute it to some unique event going on in their lives at the time, or some unfortunate accident – for example that someone had slipped something into their drink. Believing this, they do not think their breakdown will ever occur again and see no need to take any drugs.

Another view which some sufferers hold is that taking drugs to overcome a psychological problem is a sign of weakness. Some people with schizophrenia feel that they should be able to combat the condition themselves without the need of medication.

Sometimes the experience of being psychotic is such a

powerful one and even, in some rare cases, a pleasant one, that returning to the normal world is a complete let-down. One of my patients believed that he was about to win £1 million on the Pools when he was at the height of his illness. When he was treated and no longer believed this, he felt utterly despondent and only wanted to return to his former happy, albeit psychotic, state.

For all these reasons, including their past experiences of side-effects, many people with schizophrenia are reluctant to take medication when they are well. There is the natural question that if they are well, why should they take drugs? My usual answer to this is to compare schizophrenia with diabetes. If a person with diabetes does not take insulin, even if he or she feels well, he or she will become ill at some time in the future. This line of argument sometimes works as the last resort.

ALTERNATIVE DRUGS

You will see from Tables 1 and 2 (*pages 127 and 128*) that there are a substantial number of neuroleptics for the treatment of schizophrenia. However, other drugs may be prescribed for the sufferer for a variety of reasons, not all of which are necessarily logical good reasons. Do check with the consultant psychiatrist or the GP, therefore, that the drug prescribed is a true neuroleptic and, if it is not, the reason for its prescription.

Non-drug Treatments

I cannot emphasize enough that drug treatment, with the correct drugs at the correct dosages, is the only effective treatment for schizophrenia. Any other treatment may serve to improve the quality of life in those for whom drug treatment is either totally or only partially effective, but is very unlikely to be anything like as effective as the most suitable antischizophrenic drug administered at its correct dose.

OTHER BIOLOGICAL TREATMENTS

Electroconvulsive Therapy (ECT)

As I have said, there is no justification, in my view and in the view of most psychiatrists, for any biological treatment other than drug treatment with the drugs listed in Tables 1 and 2. Some psychiatrists still recommend electroconvulsive therapy (ECT) for schizophrenia, but I believe that there is no justification for this. Other biological treatments (for example insulin coma, mentioned at the start of this chapter) are now, fortunately, no longer used in the treatment of schizophrenia.

Special Diets / Vitamin Supplements

You may have heard about special diets to combat schizophrenia, or the use of vitamins or herbs as possible remedies. None of these biological treatments does any harm, but no one has been able to show in a carefully controlled, rigorously scientific study that they do any good.

Dietary change and megavitamin therapy are certainly no substitute for carefully supervised, correct antischizophrenic drug treatment.

It should be noted in this context that all of us benefit from a well-balanced diet drawing on the four main food groups (protein in the form of meat, fish and eggs; dairy products including milk and cheese; vegetables and fruit; cereals, pulses and grains for fibre). No one food should be favoured. It should also be noted that some vitamins and some herbs can cause unpleasant and potentially dangerous effects if taken in very large amounts.

PSYCHOTHERAPY

I am sometimes asked by a worried or dissatisfied relative if I offer psychotherapy for schizophrenia. The answer I give, because I know what is behind the request, is yes and no. In fact, it is more no than yes. The real reason behind the request is, usually, a distaste for drug therapy. The relative has the same reservations about drug treatment as the sufferer him- or herself (already discussed in this chapter). I tell them that schizophrenia is an illness and we are lucky in this era that an effective drug has been found for it. However, I also explain that I will try to understand as carefully as I can what the sufferer from schizophrenia is thinking or experiencing, and, in this way, when he or she recovers from the acute episode, endeavour to help with the personal and social problems that having had a severe breakdown entail.

This sort of therapy is what is called supportive psychotherapy. It is talking to sufferers in such a way that they feel that you understand or are trying to understand their problems, and that you will help them surmount any consequences that arise from their illness. Some psychiatrists, and some GPs, are good at it; others less so.

It helps sufferers enormously for them to know that you do not regard them as malingerers or frauds, as that is how some people regard people with schizophrenia. Giving advice on how to claim state benefits or applying for jobs, with the reassurance that the psychiatrist will do everything in his or her power to help with employment and with benefits bureaucracy – all part of supportive therapy – may be a great relief. Simply regarding people with schizophrenia as normal people who have had the misfortune to suffer a distressing illness which few people understand – which is the truth – may in itself give them great confidence.

A consultant may also be able to smooth over family concerns about the sufferer or persuade an employer to take him or her back. A diagnosis of schizophrenia means that a whole host of negative thoughts run through the minds of family, friends and employers. Most of these hark back to the pre-chlorpromazine era, however; remarkably few lay-people know how much the prospect for people with schizophrenia has altered in the past few decades.

There is a tendency to think of psychotherapy as a mystical process in which someone with charisma and a deep understanding of human nature can set to rights one's past and make one feel at ease with anything that life may have in store. There are such therapists and there are people who benefit from this, but this has nothing to do with schizophrenia. Professional psychotherapists, whether they be doctors or lay-people with a specialist training in helping troubled people, rarely treat people with schizophrenia. They are more concerned with people who have no psychiatric disorder at all, but who are at odds with their lives.

Schizophrenia cannot be cured by psychotherapy, whatever technique is used – Freudian psychoanalysis, Jungian psychotherapy, or any of the modern psychotherapies. These include Rogerian psychotherapy, Gestalt therapy, psychodrama, primal scream therapy, transactional analysis, Reichian therapy, bioenergetics, rolfing, behavioural psychotherapy, cognitive therapy and EST. Of all these, only supportive psychotherapy, behaviour therapy and cognitive therapy can prove useful in the treatment of schizophrenia – provided only that they are allied to a drug programme.

The only role for psychotherapy in schizophrenia is an ancillary one – empathizing with the sufferer's experiences in the acute, psychotic phase and supporting the sufferer in the aftermath. This can be done by anyone who is a good listener, professional or otherwise. What is needed is a good understanding of the condition of schizophrenia and not a dogmatic, systematized view of how life should be lived and emotions expressed. Some therapists, particularly practitioners of the modern therapies, have little understanding of and no professional training in the nature of schizophrenia and, in addition, are committed to promoting their favoured therapy, despite the fact that such therapy cannot help people with schizophrenia.

Family Therapy

Counselling sessions involving the whole family are sometimes advised as an adjunct to drug treatment. The idea behind this is that certain attitudes that family members take towards a relative with schizophrenia may exacerbate the condition and even cause a return of symptoms. I am not convinced that anything a family may say or do can cause a recurrence of a florid or full-blown breakdown, although some psychiatrists believe this.

Two attitudes in particular, however, may be detrimental: one is over-involvement by a key family member in the life of a schizophrenic – rarely leaving him alone, wanting to know what he is doing all the time, organizing his every activity, and so on; the other is being overcritical of his behaviour – nagging, belittling. Neither of these attitudes is helpful to anybody, whether he is ill or not, and indeed sufferers from depression or anorexia nervosa, for example, also fare worse if their relatives adopt these attitudes.

If the psychiatrist believes that the family is holding up a schizophrenic's progress in this way, he or she may call a meeting of the family to try and thrash out the problems. It is no criticism of a relative if this happens. Living with someone with schizophrenia can be very demanding and frustrating, and the psychiatrist can help sort out which of the annoying things the person does are part of the illness and have to be tolerated, and which things are not part of the illness and can be worked on and, hopefully, modified.

Behaviour Therapy

This form of therapy is an organized way of identifying troublesome behaviour and trying to eliminate it by the use of simple principles of how people learn and unlearn things. It is most commonly practised in the treatment of neuroses – particularly anxiety and phobias. If someone has agoraphobia – is frightened of going too far from home in case she faints and makes a fool of herself, for example – then you treat this as if it were a bad habit. Such people have learned incorrectly that they are likely to collapse and feel ashamed in busy shops or crowded trains. It may have happened once or twice but it is most unlikely to occur every time. The treatment is strongly to encourage sufferers to remain wherever they are when the anxiety comes on, rather than heading straight for home. By facing the feared situation a number of times and sticking with the anxiety each time, which almost always passes in under 30 minutes, they relearn sensible behaviour.

In the case of schizophrenia this approach is useless for the condition as a whole because the abnormal behaviour is erratic and irrational. It is not simply a bad habit. However, there is sometimes a place for behaviour therapy in those people whose schizophrenia has failed to respond to drug treatment, or for elderly schizophrenics whose illness began in the pre-chlorpromazine era and so has become chronic and resistant to drugs. Behaviour therapy is carried out by clinical psychologists who are trained to analyse abnormal behaviour; this would usually be done only for hospital in-patients. Poor self-care (an unwashed or untidy state), senseless shouting or aggressive behaviour might be singled out and be the target for the behavioural approach. The person would be rewarded, by praise and perhaps by treats, for showing less of the unwanted behaviour, and mildly punished, by withholding prized items, if the behaviour continued.

However, as I have said, this approach can only be regarded as ancillary; it is not an effective treatment unless supported by the correct medication.

Self-Control

It may seem paradoxical to include self-control in the list of treatments for a condition where the 'self' is out of control. Recovery from an episode of schizophrenia, however, is not always complete. The person regains touch with reality but is still troubled by occasional hallucinations or strange ideas. It is in such cases that one can teach ways of dealing with this which allow a better quality of life. This is what is meant by self-control – psychologists call it cognitive therapy. The word cognition covers attention, perception and thinking, and cognitive therapy is therefore a method of instructing someone to reorganize and cope with unwanted perceptions and thoughts.

The most common symptoms of schizophrenia to persist when all others have cleared up are auditory hallucinations. Moreover, sufferers can sometimes recognize certain activities or emotions which trigger these off. Peter, for example, noticed that when he was alone in a quiet room his voices would appear, but when in company or in noisy surroundings they would completely disappear. Margaret found the opposite was true for her: any noise, particularly speech on the radio, would bring her voices on, and she would have to retire to bed in complete silence to be rid of them. A patient of Peter Slade, a British psychologist who has taken an interest in the nature of auditory hallucinations, noticed that heavy physical activity such as clearing his path of snow was a trigger for their appearance. Another of Peter Slade's patients found that, whenever he became irritable, anxious or miserable, the voices would get worse.

It is not just voices that can come and go in this way; strange ideas can behave like this, too. Walter, for example, had been fairly well for 10 years and living a normal life, but he had what he called 'bad days' every month or so. At such times he felt uneasy in the street as if 'people were having a go' at him. He had learned that the best thing to do was to stay in bed all day if this happened, and next day he would be fine again.

Self-control, therefore, involves discovering, if possible, any moods, activities or environmental stimuli that bring on the symptoms, and then using this knowledge to reduce or eliminate them. Quite simple techniques such as wearing headphones connected to a portable radio may do the trick. A psychologist in Birmingham, Paul Green, recommended the use of a single ear plug in one or other ear. The rationale for this is the idea of functional imbalance between the two hemispheres which I discussed in Chapter 5. Green believed that auditory hallucinations were the result of the central hearing mechanisms in the two hemispheres getting out of phase, and that by shutting off one of them the voices would diminish. This explanation is probably incorrect, but there is no harm in trying the ear-plug technique. It is simple and cheap.

Self-control also involves adopting a certain attitude towards abnormal perceptions and ideas. The curious thing about schizophrenia is not only why the symptoms occur in the first place but why they are so insistent. They preoccupy the sufferer to the exclusion of everything else. Obviously, if what the voice is saying is terrifying – telling you, for example, that the Mafia are out to kill you – then it is no wonder that you are preoccupied. But quite often the messages are benign, yet they still dominate the mind. Simon, although otherwise well, conceived the idea that the man next door was forever staring at him in a peculiar way. He could not think of anything else, and would turn up at the hospital night and day asking for reassurance and an explanation for this. His concern about the matter could not be assuaged and he finally moved house.

The ideal aim of self-control would be to treat such ideas as silly or a nuisance and not let them take over and ruin your life. For most sufferers, delusions and hallucinations do not just suddenly evaporate as the episode clears, but get less insistent and are pushed more and more to the back of the mind. Some sufferers can find a way of doing this earlier than others, some never seem able to do it.

SOCIAL TREATMENTS

Occupational Therapy

There are several reasons for encouraging people with schizophrenia to engage in occupational therapy while they are in hospital. The first follows on from the previous section on self-control. It is an opportunity to do something practical to take their minds off their preoccupations with delusions and hallucinations. Another is to build up confidence that their minds are not completely stagnant but can cope with a whole range of tasks. Finally, it can act as a first step towards returning to a normal everyday existence. Sufferers can practise skills that they need in their job – typing or woodwork, for example; or they can branch out and do things like pottery and painting which they haven't done since childhood and thereby may discover talents they didn't know they had.

Other Sources of Help

THE ROLE OF PROFESSIONALS IN TREATMENT

Nowadays, the treatment of schizophrenia is not just a matter between psychiatrist, nurse and patient. Most UK hospitals have a team of professionals, each of whom contributes to some aspect of the treatment.

At the weekly ward round in hospital, for example, the sufferer may be ushered into a room of seven or eight people. This can be a daunting experience at first, but as patients get to know the members of the team they will find the approach an advantage rather than a disadvantage.

- The *consultant psychiatrist* is in charge of the team and overall care. A psychiatrist is a fully qualified doctor of medicine who has then become additionally qualified in psychiatry. A consultant psychiatrist is one who has practised as a psychiatrist for several years and been appointed to the post of consultant.
- There will be *one or two junior psychiatrists* at different stages in their careers, who will have a more day-to-day involvement than the consultant.
- The most closely involved of all are the *nurses*, who work shifts. In some wards sufferers will be allocated a particular nurse who will act as the first person to whom they can turn. This nurse will negotiate a daily programme of activity and encourage patients to review their progress at least weekly.
- There will usually be a *social worker* attached to the team, with whom sufferers can discuss immediate social concerns such as the care of their children while they are in hospital or longer-term concerns such as housing.

- There may be a *clinical psychologist*, with special knowledge of how to teach self-control techniques (cognitive therapy) such as those discussed in the previous section.
- There will also be an *occupational therapist* who will discuss with patients a programme of occupational therapy during their stay in hospital.

Rehabilitation

Any illness disturbs the natural flow of someone's life. If it had never happened, who knows what the person might have achieved. An illness such as appendicitis causes only minor hiccups, perhaps ruining the family's summer holiday or causing temporary loss of earnings for the self-employed. Of course, if it happens before some important event – a crucial exam or business deal – it may have consequences far beyond its severity.

Schizophrenia, however, has a much greater capacity for disrupting someone's life than this. First of all, it tends to occur at a crucial stage in life – the uneasy transition between adolescence and adulthood. Secondly, it affects the mind rather than the body, causing changes in the most deep-seated beliefs that people can have – who they are, how the world is, and so on. Thirdly, it is often a long drawn-out affair: months or years may elapse before it is correctly diagnosed and properly treated. This causes sufferers and their families to make secondary adjustments to their lifestyle which are often harder to undo than the actual effects of the illness. Fourthly, even when people recover from the acute psychotic phase, the effects of the illness may not end there. There may be recurrences if the medication is not well supervised, and there may be sporadic psychotic symptoms, such as hallucinations, which persist despite the most tightly controlled drug regime.

Finally, there is a minority in whom the illness leaves behind residual problems of unsociability, lack of drive and impaired concentration.

Rehabilitation means tackling all the residual problems that sufferers have when they emerge from the acute stage of an illness. This involves attention to interpersonal problems, accommodation requirements, job prospects and preventing, if possible, any return of the illness. There are particular problems in each of these areas for someone with schizophrenia.

INTERPERSONAL PROBLEMS

The interpersonal problems that people with schizophrenia suffer derive from several sources. Some are the result of altered attitudes on the part of others who bore the brunt of the sufferer's irrational actions during the acute illness. One of my patients, for example, had sexually molested his favourite sister because he thought she was a prostitute. He and she needed help to re-establish their relationship after discussing how his behaviour was the result of his delusions. Sometimes, interpersonal problems existed even before the illness developed. A sense of social unease and awkwardness may have been part of a schizoid personality (discussed at the end of Chapter 2 and in Chapter 4). The attention paid to the psychotic episode may bring the personality disorder to light. Alternatively, the illness itself may leave the sufferer with residual symptoms of unsociability, lack of initiative and poor concentration once the florid, or full-blown, delusions and hallucinations recede. In this case it is usually the relatives, rather than the sufferer, who complain of this.

I have found that the best approach in all these circumstances is to encourage the person to become more sociable – to join clubs, to take up adult educational activities and to persevere in his or her job or job applications. If patients with schizophrenia complain bitterly about problems in getting on with other people, I regard this as a good sign as it shows that their schizoid nature or residual unsociability is not so deep that they cannot appreciate their social problems. If they wish to improve what are known as 'social skills', I refer them to the clinical psychologist working in my team or to the occupational therapist, if they are still in-patients. Many occupational therapists run groups for improving social skills.

Schizophrenia affects the very mental functions that form the basis for normal social behaviour. For example, there are certain unwritten rules about how long you look people in the eye when talking to them, or how much you disclose about your personal life, and so on. You cannot learn these rules from a book. You can only know them through experience. People with schizophrenia in a psychotic phase no longer know these rules, and seem to be poor at applying them even when apparently well. Social skills therapy – teaching the right length of eye contact or appropriate 'getting to know people' techniques, for example – are often recommended for those with schizophrenia, but it should be appreciated that the sufferer is trying to cure, with this sort of therapy, the very basis for the condition and, therefore, may be disappointed.

FAMILY RELATIONSHIPS
Another aspect of interpersonal problems lies within the family. I have dealt with this when discussing family therapy earlier in this chapter. I should stress that this is a very delicate issue. There is nothing worse than having to cope with the burden of living with an inadequately treated schizophrenic, and then having a psychiatrist tell you that it is partly your fault and forcing you to have to go through a painful soul-searching exercise in how you did this or that wrong when your child was a certain age. Family therapy should be mutually beneficial, to you

and the sufferer, and should be constructive rather than the focus of future rows. It should also be noted in this context that faulty upbringing and family tensions are never the cause of schizophrenia, as we saw in Chapter 5.

WHERE TO LIVE?

People with schizophrenia have accommodation problems like anyone else. The particular issue is whether they do better remaining at home with their family, branching out on their own, or living in some supervised hostel. My own opinion is that from a family's point of view having a relative with schizophrenia is no different from having any difficult family member to cope with. What one does depends on the resources of love and commitment that have been built up over the years. Sometimes the behaviour of someone with schizophrenia can be so outrageous that all this can be destroyed overnight. This is one of the tragedies of the condition. In many cases, however, unnatural behaviour can be forgiven and forgotten if it is appreciated that it is out of character.

As a last resort there are several organizations that cater for single people who have had breakdowns. These are listed in Appendix B.

EMPLOYMENT

In the 1960s and 1970s one of the main elements in the rehabilitation of people with schizophrenia was to set them to work in a hospital workshop designed to simulate real work conditions. The organizers of the workshop would take in light industrial tasks such as packing or printing. The aim was to prepare the recovered schizophrenic for the real 'job world' outside the hospital. The rationale behind this was that jobs were so plentiful that employers would take on anyone, regardless of his or her employment record. In fact, the prospects of employment in certain parts of the country are now so poor that any hint of a breakdown in an applicant for a job is a virtual bar to employment.

There are two solutions to this problem. One is to accept that the employment situation is such that some people with schizophrenia will never either attain or retain a good job. I should say that I may be unduly pessimistic about this because my patients mainly come from a high unemployment area of Britain, albeit in the prosperous south. But, if you study the trends in employment prospects for the rest of the century, it is clear that unskilled jobs will be less and less in demand. Only those people with the social skills to create their own clientele will be able to command easy work. The second solution for people with schizophrenia is, on this analysis, to accept that they may well be officially unemployable, but to seek appropriate and absorbing leisure activities that improve their quality of life.

DAY CENTRES

The local authorities in Britain provide day centres for people who have been psychiatrically ill, and these may suit some people with schizophrenia. They can go there between 10 in the morning and 4 in the afternoon, and the staff run group meetings and provide them with occupational therapy and light industrial tasks. You can find out about these in Great Britain from your local social services department.

After discharge from hospital the supervision of medication and the overall care of a schizophrenic should be in the hands of the consultant psychiatrist who was looking after him or her in hospital. Sometimes a general practitioner may share the care with the psychiatrist, but in general I believe that schizophrenia is too specialized a subject to be left entirely in the hands of a general practitioner, as well as for a number of other reasons which include decisions about medication and the difficulties of spotting the early signs of an impending relapse. The psychiatrist may call on the services of a community psychiatric nurse, if one is available, to monitor progress at home. If it is thought better that the sufferer live in a hostel, then the social worker will liaise with the staff of the hostel to make sure everything is running smoothly.

Where to Obtain Treatment

Schizophrenia is usually treated in hospital (particularly if this is the first full-blown episode of the illness), just as any other serious illness is. Schizophrenia is a serious illness that, in its acute phases, cannot usually be managed at home. In the same way, most cases of stomach ache can be managed at home, but if the cause is appendicitis, for example, or a perforated ulcer, then the person has to be treated in hospital.

IN HOSPITAL

Admission to hospital is an important event in anyone's life. One is removed from the safety of the home environment and forced into the company of people whom one doesn't know and may not particularly want to know.

I nevertheless believe that people with schizophrenia should be admitted to hospital in the first episode of their illness, for the following reasons.

Firstly, it is imperative to make the correct diagnosis from the beginning, and the joint observations of nurses, doctors, psychologists and occupational therapists are extremely useful. This is not to underestimate the value of a relative's observations. However, what the sufferer says or does in front of a stranger, particularly if it occurs in front of several strangers, may resolve a diagnostic dilemma.

Secondly, hospital admission allows the psychiatrist to carry out certain investigations which cannot easily be done as an outpatient – for example, scans and blood tests.

Thirdly, and most importantly, the psychiatric team can evaluate the sufferer's response to medication, day by day and, hopefully, by the end of their stay have them on the best drug at the right dose. As an outpatient this may take ages, and a short two- or three-week admission may save the sufferer months of misery.

If all goes well, the admission should not exceed a month and, in the mean time, occupational therapy may introduce sufferers to new skills or help them to discover talents that they did not know they possessed.

Relatives should, ideally, be told seven days in advance that the sufferer is to be discharged, unless the sufferer asks for the family not to be advised.

The question of compulsory admission to hospital is discussed in the second part of Chapter 7, under Getting the Best Out of the System.

CARE IN THE COMMUNITY

You may have heard the phrase 'community care for people with schizophrenia'. These days this is no mere slogan for 'cheap care for people with schizophrenia'. Care in the community was first mooted during the 1960s and 1970s when the introduction of neuroleptic drugs (described at the start of this chapter) dramatically reduced the number of people with schizophrenia who needed to be in hospital for the rest of their lives. It was then assumed by the Government, and by a few psychiatrists and some psychologists, that no one with schizophrenia needed long-term or even medium-term hospital treatment. Hospital places were, accordingly, cut drastically.

Today, it is quite clear that some people with schizophrenia (between a fifth and a tenth) cannot cope with the outside world and do need a place in a hospital for a long period. Such sufferers, whether their illness is resistant to neuroleptic drugs or whether they just cannot be persuaded to take their drugs, cannot be ignored. Unfortunately, the provision for these people is inadequate. In the wake of several incidents in Britain in the early 1990s involving people with schizophrenia who harmed themselves or killed other people, the Government has introduced certain statutory guidelines about care in the community. These include a 'supervision register' and a 'care programme approach', whereby anyone with schizophrenia who is deemed at risk in some way will be provided with a key worker to monitor his or her activities. It is too early to say how this will all turn out.

PROBLEMS IN OBTAINING TREATMENT

If you, as a relative or a friend of someone with schizophrenia, experience problems in obtaining treatment for the sufferer or problems with the treatment itself, do read carefully the second part of Chapter 7, Getting the Best Out of the System. Most of these sorts of problems can usually be straightened out, providing that you know where to go for help.

7

COPING WITH SOMEONE WITH SCHIZOPHRENIA

In the last chapter I dealt with the official treatment of schizophrenia. But, as a relative or a friend of someone with schizophrenia, you will know that numerous problems crop up on a
day-to-day basis and that a psychiatrist or other involved professional cannot be on the spot to sort these out. You may feel
that you can deal with most of these as they occur, but you
may benefit from some guidelines if, as often happens, a schizophrenic's behaviour and attitudes in some situations are puzzling and perverse.

Before the introduction of chlorpromazine in the 1950s,
the majority of people with schizophrenia had to spend their
entire lives in hospital because their behaviour was so unman-
ageable at home. Now, fewer than 10 per cent are so disturbed
that they need continuous hospital care. However, even with
the most careful attention to medication some people with
schizophrenia, although not ill enough to be in hospital, will
continue to show signs of their condition. The first part of this
chapter is mainly about how to manage those people who have
recovered from their acute schizophrenic breakdown but are
not entirely normal and self-sufficient.

Some of the problems you will encounter stem directly

from lingering signs of the illness itself. Some result from the consequences of the sufferer having been ill. Others have more to do with your own and the sufferer's concern that he or she might become ill again. Regardless of the source of the problems, there is no doubt that relatives now have to bear the brunt of much of the caring for someone with schizophrenia, when once this was the sole job of psychiatrists and nurses.

The remarkable improvement in outcome for people with schizophrenia since the pre-chlorpromazine era has, to some extent, made life harder for caring relatives. Before 1950 it was almost impossible for even the most devoted relative to look after the sufferer at home. Now, with closure of the large mental hospitals and lack of government resources to provide alternative hospital or hostel care, the burden of caring for someone with schizophrenia falls increasingly on relatives.

The purpose of the first part of this chapter is to help you cope with the ups and downs of living with someone who has schizophrenia but who is comparatively well at the moment. It may also help you to look back to Chapter 6 and read the section entitled Rehabilitation (*page 150*), which includes information about day centres.

The second part of this chapter shows you how you can make the most of the services available to you if the sufferer becomes ill again, schizophrenia and the law, and details of the lay support organizations dedicated to helping people with schizophrenia and their friends and relatives.

Understanding Your Schizophrenic Relative or Friend

The golden rule, in my view, is to treat your schizophrenic relative or friend to some extent as if he or she were a normal person who is both eccentric and unsociable, bearing in mind of course that he or she has a disabling illness. An understanding of the nature of schizophrenia (*see Chapters 1 and 2*) and of the need for continued medication as determined by the consultant (*see Chapter 6*) are invaluable if you are to help and support your relative or friend effectively. What then are the most common problems you will encounter in the quiescent, or convalescent, stage?

UNSOCIAL BEHAVIOUR

Most of your problems will arise because the person's attitude to life is different from those of the rest of the family. Sufferers are inclined to be less sociable, less ambitious and less likely to follow the usual pattern of life – job, marriage, social gatherings. They may appear lazy, selfish and withdrawn when measured against the expectations of a society that prizes financial and social success above all else. Their inclination is for a more subdued life, their interests more intellectual and private. If you can accept that this is so and that there is no point in forcing someone with schizophrenia into a conventional mould, then half the battle will be over. In fact, their attitude to life is in some ways the ideal encouraged by some religions. However, in our modern society in which we are all expected to pay our way, it can be irritating and frustrating. It is a curious fact that, although schizophrenia occurs in all parts of the world at the same rate, the outcome in developing countries is actually better than it is in developed countries. This may have something to do with a more tolerant attitude towards schizophrenia in so-called 'under-developed' cultures.

Lying in bed all day or refusing to help with household chores is going too far, of course, and you must and can ensure that your relative will observe simple family rules. What you cannot rely on is their wholehearted participation at family gatherings, their ability to initiate social outings on their own, or their capacity to go out and get a job and keep it. At worst you may feel that your relative or friend is a passenger in your life, but if you can take a broader view — that not everyone has to be a success in life — you will find that they are easier to live with. In many ways someone with schizophrenia may complement a family of extroverts and strivers. It will help both you and your relative or friend if you encourage social activity with outings and so on. Try, too, to get other relatives and friends to help; does, for example, one of your relatives or friends share any of the sufferer's interests? Try to involve the rest of your family if you can, and remember that you will benefit from a rest from caring for your relative.

IRRITATING HABITS

Living together with someone whose habits irritate you can be a trial for all concerned. Leaving the cap off the toothpaste tube, snoring, or eating noisily can all be annoying in the extreme for some. Another set of habits may irritate someone else.

You may come to accept the fact that your relative or friend does not want to join in family activities or that they do not pull their weight in jobs around the house. But, when it comes to eating habits, sleep patterns and personal hygiene, you may feel you have to draw the line.

If they grab food, eat like an animal or demand massive helpings and are getting fat, then all this should be tackled as if you were training a child in table manners. Your relative or friend may have forgotten how to behave at table because of laxity in these matters while they were in hospital, or may not realize the effect it has on other people, simply because they are in a world of their own so much of the time.

If they sleep till lunch-time and then stay up half the night playing music, then this pattern must be broken. They may ask for sleeping tablets because they can't get to sleep at night when in fact they sleep half the day and take no exercise. You may have to devise a simple daily routine – breakfast at such and such an hour followed by tasks, errands and activities – to get them to return to more normal sleeping habits. It may be that the dose of medication they are on is too high; you should inform your psychiatrist if they are sleeping too much overall or for noticeably longer than they used to.

They may show little interest in clothes, but this does not condone sloppy personal hygiene. It may be that they missed out on the stage in adolescence when teenagers start to take an interest in their appearance in order to impress and be attractive. It may be that they are so used to staying in that they have rarely experienced the joy of dressing up and wearing something different. Whatever the reason, you should take a firm line.

You may find that cajoling and arguing about these matters is to no avail. In this case you will have to resort to more drastic measures. In hospital, if patients go back to bed after breakfast for no good reason, after several warnings we simply lock their door while they are at breakfast so that they cannot go back to bed. If, like a woman in our ward recently, they gobble down three helpings of dinner and then vomit it afterwards, we refuse to let them have second helpings. You have to devise rewards and punishments to get rid of bad habits.

ADDICTIONS

Most people with schizophrenia are heavy smokers. This can be a source of much family tension if the rest of the members of the household are non-smokers. Why they smoke so much nobody knows. It may be boredom or it may be their way of improving the dulling of the senses brought about by the medication. It is unlikely that you will get your relative or friend to give up, but you can use the addiction to your advantage by rationing cigarettes as an incentive to develop more acceptable eating, sleeping and personal habits.

Alcohol is rarely a problem for people who have schizophrenia. In a recent study of drinking habits among patients with a variety of different psychiatric conditions, those with schizophrenia drank less than any other group of patients. Perhaps the reason for this is that drinking, for most people who are not alcoholics, is a social activity, and people who have schizophrenia, who are by nature as well as because of the symptoms of the illness unsocial, will not enjoy it. In fact, you could encourage them to be more sociable by suggesting that they go out for a drink.

What about illicit drugs, 'street drugs' as they are sometimes called? These are harmful to everyone but probably more so for people who have schizophrenia. It is very unlikely that these drugs actually cause schizophrenia in those who were not predisposed to it by virtue of their genetic make-up or latent brain disorganization. However, the hallucinogenic ones such as LSD ('acid') and stimulants such as amphetamine ('speed') can certainly precipitate a recurrence in someone whose illness is in a dormant phase. These drugs may also possibly cause it to begin earlier than it would have done. Cannabis ('marijuana', 'hashish', 'pot', 'dope') is probably the most commonly used street drug in developed countries. Experts disagree about whether it can cause a psychosis that outlives the actual intoxication with the drug. I am not convinced it can, as I have never seen a case, but, as cannabis has mind-altering properties, I strongly advise anyone with schizophrenia who admits to trying it never to take it again. Unfortunately, its use is so common among young people that my advice is rarely heeded.

INABILITY TO HOLD DOWN A JOB OR COURSE OF STUDY

Some people with schizophrenia manage against all the odds to hold down a job, to get a new one with better prospects or to complete their university degree or higher training course. This is the exception, sadly, rather than the rule. The job careers of most people with schizophrenia usually follow one of these patterns:

First, there are those whose illness begins early, in their late teens or early twenties, preceded by a history of erratic employment or frequent changes of college course. After their recovery from the acute psychosis they may try one or two courses or jobs, but, despite good control of their illness with medication, they cannot settle down in anything and become permanently unemployed within a few years.

A second pattern is again seen in those whose illness strikes when they are in their late teens or twenties, but in this case it is preceded by a good educational or work record right up to a few weeks before their first admission to hospital. After discharge, when comparatively well, they try to take up their course or job where they left off. Unfortunately, they may find it hard going and then give it up. They are more persevering than the previous group and tend to chop and change jobs throughout their twenties, thirties and even forties. Sometimes they stay with one job for a year or two, usually less. The jobs are below what would have been predicted for them before they became ill. They tend to go in for portering, cleaning, gardening or delivery jobs.

Another pattern is seen in those whose illness occurs later, in their thirties, preceded by a well-established career or trade or clerical position. On recovery these people try to return to their previous job but they rarely prosper despite a lenient attitude by their employers. They leave or are forced to take early retirement on medical grounds, and rarely work again.

Although job prospects for the sufferer from schizophrenia may appear bleak from what I have just said, it is unfortunately true. It is better that you know this and not try too hard to fix up jobs here and there for them and then be disappointed. It is not that people with schizophrenia are lazy or job-shy. Many of them try time and again but fail the interview or, if they get past that, get the sack for poor time-keeping or slowness. They are at a grave disadvantage, of course, when applying for a job because most application forms contain a question asking if the applicant has ever had 'trouble with their nerves'. If they answer yes they may not be short-listed; if they answer no and the truth comes out later they may be dismissed. Another reason for their poor job performance is their general dislike of the social side of work. They may not be able to enter the camaraderie, in-jokes and leg-pulling that goes on and hence may feel and indeed may be ostracized.

An ideal job for someone who has recovered from the acute stage of the illness is one that involves a minimum of social contact. The reason they drift down the employment ladder is not so much that they are intellectually less able than others but that they are socially less skilful. Running messages, gardening or cleaning can be carried out successfully without the need for too much human interaction. In all job centres throughout Britain there is someone known as a Disablement Resettlement Officer whose role is to help people with mental or physical disabilities look for a job.

DISLIKE OF MEDICATION

You may find that one of the biggest trials is your relative's or friend's attitude to medication. I touched on some of the reasons for this throughout the last chapter (*see particularly What Are the Side-effects?*). Unless sufferers are acutely psychotic the reasons are all understandable: the desire to overcome their illness on their own; the fear that they will become drug addicts; dislike of side-effects; and the belief that they were not really ill but only distressed by some event in their lives.

You will have to identify the precise reason why your relative or friend is reluctant to take medication and then tackle it using all your knowledge of the person to counter any arguments. You will need to be convinced yourself that medication is essential. I hope that this book and your own experience of the relationship between periods of improvement and regular medication will be sufficient. The psychiatrist looking after your relative should respond to your observations that one drug causes side-effects, another is better but the dose is too high, and so on, and change the medication accordingly.

As a final resort, if someone with schizophrenia refuses medication which you know has helped in the past, and is now deteriorating under your very eyes, you should inform his or her psychiatrist. If the psychiatrist cannot persuade your relative or friend to take the medication, then the question of a compulsory order for treatment, a 'Section', then arises – this is discussed later in this chapter under Schizophrenia and the Law. A compulsory order for treatment is unfortunate for all concerned, but you should remember that schizophrenia not only affects the sufferer's perceptions and ideas about the world, but affects his or her judgement of what is a good phase in life and what is not. You can argue till the cows come home that they were undoubtedly better off on medication, but they may refuse to, or be unable to, accept this.

ECCENTRIC PURSUITS

You may feel annoyed and puzzled that, whereas someone with schizophrenia refuses to participate in family life and has a disastrous series of jobs, they can nevertheless apply themselves with immense gusto and ingenuity to some unusual task. One of my patients, for example, spent all his time constructing geometrical shapes out of cardboard until he had amassed hundreds of three-dimensional pentagons, hexagons, and the like. Another would read the dictionary from cover to cover looking for words that accurately described the current political system in Britain. Some become fitness fanatics, others try to learn languages for which they have no use.

There is no point, in my view, feeling annoyed about their interest in these pursuits, although it may be difficult not to. Most of the topics that they choose reflect the schizophrenic's natural tendency to intellectualize life and to divorce themselves from social endeavours. You should encourage their interests as you might golf or badminton in a workaholic businessman. A person with schizophrenia, even when comparatively well, is often a frustrated intellectual. They have the ability to delve into the secrets of life, but they lack the knowledge as to which line to take and how to present their discoveries. A patient of mine, for example, spent years examining every specimen of urine that he produced in the hope of finding the secret of life. Obviously, this is going too far, and will be very annoying to the rest of the family. In general, however, eccentric activities and behaviour should be encouraged, as they provide leisure activity, albeit of an unusual kind.

FRANKLY MAD BEHAVIOUR

So far I have dealt with behaviour and attitudes that may occur in people with schizophrenia who are comparatively well. Their acute symptoms have been eradicated with medication and only their personality problems remain. Some schizophrenia sufferers, however, remain mildly psychotic, or mad, despite the most careful supervision of their medication. They are not ill enough to be in hospital, but their hallucinations and strange ideas are a sufficient nuisance to disturb them and their family and friends.

The first approach to take is to consult with the schizophrenic's psychiatrist as to whether the drug regime should be changed. Recently, for example, someone with schizophrenia was referred to me by a colleague for a second opinion because he had not improved with very high doses of fluphenazine (Modecate). I substituted flupenthixol (Depixol) at moderate doses but he continued to experience unpleasant voices and I referred him to a clinical psychologist colleague for self-control or cognitive therapy (*see Chapter 6*). This had little effect, and he was admitted to hospital in his local area, where the psychiatrist put him on sulpiride (Dolmatil). His voices completely disappeared. This illustrates both the power of medication and the advantage of changing a long-standing regime if it is not effective. It does not necessarily undermine the power of psychological treatments such as cognitive therapy, as they are currently in their infancy, and, in addition, if medication changes do not work they represent the only alternative.

In general, if occasional voices or strange ideas do recur, the best approach is to regard them as obstacles on the road to recovery. Tell your relative or friend that these are the last remnants of the illness and that these ideas, etc. will more and more move to the back of their mind and cease to trouble them. Tell them that these voices can no longer exert an influence on their new self-sufficiency, and that on no account should the sufferer regard them as real. Of course, one cannot prescribe reality for someone, but, in the context of the fading influence of a psychosis or full-blown episode of schizophrenia, one can try to speed up the process of encouraging 'normal' reality in this way.

UNREALISTIC HOPES AND EXPECTATIONS

A final set of problems concerns the gap between schizophrenics' view of their future and the view their family has of their future. It is rare that sufferers plan their future – marriage, such and such a job, children, a house and eventually retirement and satisfaction at a life well lived. You might think that this is too artificial even for a normal person, too much like a life insurance company's advert. However, most people do dream about their ideal life, even though few may achieve it. They make decisions on the basis of it, in the hope that the ideal man or woman will come along and realize their dreams. Or they marry and make the best of their lives, trying to persuade their spouse to move to this or that part of the country, to have more or no more children, or to help them make their mark in local society. It is all planned, albeit in a disorganized fashion.

Such plans are totally absent from the minds of those suffering from schizophrenia. They tend to live literally from day to day. You may ask them about marriage or future job prospects and they may answer appropriately, but it is doubtful if their answers come from a true appreciation of their situation.

In many respects people with schizophrenia behave like adolescents or romantic poets, looking forward to the day ahead without a care for the months or years beyond that. As a well-organized person this attitude may appal you, but remember that people with schizophrenia are not *in* the world as we know it, but *alongside* it. They are relatively immune to social pressures but exquisitely aware of intellectual issues that pass the rest of us by.

Getting the Best Out of the System

What do you do if you are unhappy with the care given to someone suffering from schizophrenia? Coping with a schizophrenic relative or friend is sometimes further complicated by worries about diagnosis, for example, or worries about the correct dose of drug. This part of the chapter is intended to show you how to get the best out of the system and how to make the most of the services available to you if your relative or friend becomes ill again. I am looking, in particular, at problems in the psychiatric care of your relative or friend; schizophrenia and the law (notably how the law stands on the question of compulsory admission of someone with the illness to hospital); and the lay support organizations that can help you and the sufferer.

Most of what I have to say will be true only for Great Britain, because the pattern of psychiatric care, mental health laws and lay organizations differs widely from country to country.

OFFICIAL PSYCHIATRIC CARE
In Great Britain psychiatric care is organized rigidly into sectors. If you happen to live in North Bolton or South Kensington you will have a particular psychiatrist and a particular social worker covering your area. If you and your relative hit it off with your local psychiatrist, all well and good. If you don't, you are still stuck with him or her, unless you are prepared to go privately, and this is very costly.

If you feel strongly that the care that your schizophrenic relative is receiving is inadequate, then think carefully about why this might be so before deciding on the available options.

Concern about Diagnosis
It might be that you are convinced that your psychiatrist has

made the wrong diagnosis. Some people resist the idea that their relative might have schizophrenia, and seek opinion after opinion, hoping that it is not so. This is usually short-sighted and may be detrimental to the sufferer, because there is evidence that the earlier consistent medication is started, the better the outlook. It is understandable that relatives should take this line, because the word schizophrenia has such negative associations. However, as I have tried to indicate in this book, many of the bad connotations attached to schizophrenia originate from how it was seen in the pre-chlorpromazine era. As the outlook has improved immeasurably since then, it is no longer such a dreadful label. As often happens, however, prejudice takes a long time to catch up with the truth.

You are, however, right to question the diagnosis on the basis of one opinion. Over a period of four years I was referred about 50 psychotic patients by colleagues, to give a second opinion because these patients had unaccountably failed to respond to medication. In no less than 20 of these the diagnosis was wrong – schizophrenia when it was in fact something else, and some other condition when the original, referral diagnosis was schizophrenia. The second opinion cases that I deal with tend to be difficult problems, by their very nature, but these figures indicate that even the best psychiatrist can make mistakes. I myself am continually making mistakes on the basis of one interview, because schizophrenia is such a difficult diagnosis to make.

Worries about the Medication

You may accept the diagnosis of schizophrenia but be concerned about the way your relative is being looked after. Some psychiatrists do not follow the guidelines about dosage laid out in Chapter 6. They believe that bigger doses are required. This places you in a quandary, because if you insist that your schizophrenic relative would be better off on lower doses of medication, the psychiatrist may insist on the opposite and you will lose mutual co-operation. I feel strongly about this issue, because the end result of giving too high a dose of medication is usually that the sufferer refuses to take any drugs at all and then relapses. All you can do in the first instance is point this out to your psychiatrist. As a last resort, you can ask the psychiatrist (or your GP) to arrange for a second opinion from another consultant psychiatrist.

Frustration That the Psychiatrist Is Not Doing Enough

You may feel that your relative is sometimes left untreated to do as he or she pleases through insufficient action on the part of the psychiatrist. I have been consulted by many relatives, from different parts of the country, who feel this way and who have pleaded with me to get something done. In these circumstances it is rarely the fault of the local psychiatrist, as the sufferer him- or herself refuses to accept voluntary treatment. It then becomes a legal issue, as to whether the law allows one to insist upon compulsory admission to hospital and treatment. The psychiatrist then becomes one of several people (*see Schizophrenia and the Law, below*) who must sign the relevant documents committing the person to hospital. Even if all parties agree, as you will see, there is a process of appeal; a panel of three people – the Mental Health Tribunal – is called in, on the say-so of the sufferer, and it can overturn the decision of the professionals and relatives. This panel comprises a senior lawyer, an outside psychiatrist, and a lay member.

Compulsory admission to hospital and treatment orders are, therefore, no simple solution, although they are increasingly being used because psychiatrists and relatives alike are becoming more aware of the dangers of delaying treatment.

Inadequate Follow-up and Rehabilitation

You may feel happy with the diagnosis and treatment, and confident that should the need arise your psychiatrist will do his or her utmost to ensure speedy readmission. Nevertheless, you may feel that things are stagnating, that the sufferer could be doing better.

This is a complex issue. It may be that the person is as well as can be expected, though not as well as you would like, remembering how he or she was before the illness. This situation reflects the social problems that remain in many people after the acute stage of the illness has passed (discussed in the first part of this chapter). There may, however, be genuine ways in which those with schizophrenia can be encouraged to improve themselves. All the ancillary therapies and social facilities discussed in Chapter 6 are geared towards this. You should discuss your concern with your psychiatrist, who in turn can refer you to a social worker, psychologist, counsellor, day centre supervisor or disablement resettlement officer, depending on the particular problem. Failing this you could contact your local branch of the Schizophrenia Fellowship or Mind (*see below*); they can put you in touch with facilities in your area.

WHAT YOU CAN DO

If you cannot resolve your worries about diagnosis and treatment with your local psychiatrist or find help with social rehabilitation from lay organizations like the Schizophrenia Fellowship or Mind, you can seek a second opinion. This is not a step to be taken lightly because you might irritate or alienate your local psychiatrist, whose help and co-operation you will need if readmission to hospital is required in the future. Nevertheless, you are quite entitled to do so and your general practitioner or the Schizophrenia Fellowship will probably know of a psychiatrist who is prepared to see your relative, privately or on the National Health Service. The second psychiatrist is unlikely to accept the total care of the person because he or she will have his or her own sector commitments, but will offer you an opinion about diagnosis and treatment, which can be fed back to your local psychiatrist both by the second psychiatrist and by you. If you obtain the approval of your local psychiatrist first, he or she is then more likely to be obliging.

Schizophrenia and the Law

In Britain the Mental Health Act of 1983 governs the current law on compulsory admission to hospital of people with schizophrenia, and their right to appeal against this. You should know the main Sections of the Act, your role as a relative in these, and the legal rights of the detained person.

COMPULSORY ADMISSION TO HOSPITAL
Two Sections of the Mental Health Act, Section 2 and Section 3, are the most important in the context of compulsory admission.

Section 2 allows for admission for assessment and treatment, and lasts 28 days. The form must be signed by three people – two doctors and the nearest relative or an 'approved' social worker. One of the doctors must be 'approved', which in practice means being a psychiatrist with more than three years of psychiatric experience. One of the doctors must be working outside the hospital to which the patient is admitted; this in practice means that he or she is a general practitioner or a psychiatrist from another hospital.

Both doctors have to certify that they believe that the person suffers from a 'mental disorder which warrants detention in hospital and ought to be so detained in the interests of his or her own health or safety or with a view to the protection of other persons'. This clause is variously interpreted by doctors. In practice it usually means that the person has to be psychotic, or classifiably mentally ill (*see pages 26–27*). Very rarely, psychopaths are sectioned, but only if they have committed a dreadful crime and only then to one of the few special hospitals or units for the criminally insane – now called forensic or secure hospitals or units. You cannot section an alcoholic or a neurotic person. Very rarely, an anorexic who is at death's door is sectioned. Nor can you section someone who keeps taking overdoses or keeps slashing his or her wrists unless there are other definite signs of a depressive psychosis (*see Chapter 2*). Most people who take overdoses of tablets have interpersonal problems and are not mentally ill.

It is the second part of the condition for a Section 2 which causes most problems. You cannot section people solely because they are mentally ill. You have to be convinced that their illness is likely to cause them to *harm others* or *themselves* or – and this is the controversial issue – to *be detrimental to their health*. Some psychiatrists and social workers ignore this last provision and refuse to sign the compulsory admission form unless there is definite evidence that the person has or is likely to hurt others or him- or herself. I think that this is wrong because it means that moderate to severe forms of schizophrenia may not be treated before it is too late. I have several people with schizophrenia under my care who have never been treated because I cannot persuade another doctor or a social worker to sign the form. It is not that I take a hard line on the issue of sectioning in general. Quite often, at my weekly ward round, I am appalled that an alcoholic, someone in distress or an aggressive person has been sectioned because he or she has caused a rumpus somewhere but is not, in fact, mentally ill at all.

Apart from the two doctors, the third signatory has to be the nearest relative or an approved social worker. In law the nearest relative is a spouse, child, parent, brother or sister, grandparent or grandchild, uncle or aunt, nephew or niece, in that order. If there are more than two children, then the eldest is deemed the nearest relative. However, if the person ordinarily lives with a relative lower down the legal list, that person is given precedence over those higher up. In fact, it is rare for a relative to sign the form. I advise against it because the sufferer may hold it against you in the future. In all boroughs in Great Britain there are social workers who are approved for the purpose of assessing the need for compulsory admission to hospital because they have gained experience in the matter. It is better both for the relative and the sufferer that this type of social worker signs the form.

Section 2 is mainly used for patients who, besides refusing admission when this is considered essential by all concerned, are in their first acute, psychotic episode.

Section 3 is designated as a treatment order. This is for people known to suffer from a psychotic illness and who are refusing treatment when all concerned believe it is essential. The order lasts for six months, although it can be cancelled at any stage if the sufferer improves and realizes the need for treatment. Because Section 3 constitutes a more severe step in depriving people of their liberty, there are even more safeguards than in the case of Section 2. The same number of people have to sign the form – two doctors, one 'approved' and one outside the hospital, and an approved social worker or nearest relative. But the signatories have to state *why* alternative methods of treatment – for example, as an outpatient – are not appropriate. Furthermore, after three months, if the patient is still unwilling to accept treatment, another psychiatrist nominated by the watchdog body (the Mental Health Act

Commission) has to be called in to assess the need for this treatment. The commissioner has a duty to consult two non-medical members of the ward staff, one a nurse and the other a psychologist, social worker or occupational therapist, to obtain an opinion on whether or not continuing drug treatment is essential.

Right of Appeal

On both Sections 2 and 3, detained patients have the right to appeal against detention. As soon as they are compulsorily admitted to hospital they are given a form informing them of their rights and an address to which they can write if they wish to appeal. If they decide to appeal, a Mental Health Review Tribunal is rapidly convened to hear their case. This is a panel of three people – a lawyer, a psychiatrist outside the hospital and a lay-person – who have the right to overturn the Section if they wish. The tribunal is conducted as if it were a proper case in the law courts, though without a jury. Evidence is taken from the psychiatrist, the social worker, the patient and the relative, and a judgement is then made. It is not at all a whitewash of the psychiatrist's decision. The tribunal quite often discharges someone against the hospital psychiatrist's advice.

There are other Sections, governing, for example, the compulsory admission to hospital of people with schizophrenia who have been arrested for a crime and taken to prison. There are also other routes for appeal against Sections 2 and 3, for example asking the hospital administration to convene a meeting of what are known as the Hospital Managers, a group of lay-people who are on the board of management of the hospital but who are not psychiatrists. These Hospital Managers can also overturn a Section if they wish.

The whole system is geared towards protecting an individual's rights. If anything, the pendulum has swung too far in favour of this at the expense of allowing people who are seriously ill with schizophrenia but who do not wish to be admitted to hospital to remain untreated because they are no danger to other people. This means, in effect, that law-abiding people who are seriously ill with schizophrenia are being penalized: if they were to throw a bottle through a shop window, or worse, they *would* be sectioned and thus receive the treatment that they need. Because they have not shown that they are a danger to others, they are able to resist treatment.

LAY ORGANIZATIONS

There are several organizations which have sprung up in Britain in response to the dissatisfaction by many people at the official treatment of schizophrenia. The five main ones are: The National Schizophrenia Fellowship; MIND – The National Association for Mental Health; SANE – Schizophrenia: A National Emergency; the Schizophrenia Association of Great Britain; and the Richmond Fellowship (*see Appendix B for addresses and telephone numbers*).

The National Schizophrenia Fellowship is the organization with the widest network in Great Britain and the charitable organization most used by people with schizophrenia and their relatives and friends. There are support groups all over the country. The address of the nearest group can be obtained by writing to or telephoning the central office in Kingston upon Thames (*see Appendix B*). The Fellowship produces a range of publications and maintains a number of referral lists of, for example, counsellors, consultant psychiatrists willing to give a second opinion, holiday provision, accommodation and other services. Its main role is to provide help and support for relatives of people with schizophrenia who find the illness of the sufferer puzzling and at times overwhelming.

MIND exists to campaign for the legal and social rights of all mentally ill people. Its officers were actively involved in lobbying MPs for a change in mental health legislation, and this gave rise to the 1983 Mental Health Act. In practice this Act increased the right of people with schizophrenia to appeal against compulsory detention in hospital and made psychiatrists more reluctant to 'section' people with schizophrenia (in other words, to issue a compulsory order). The organization relies on voluntary contributions from lay-people, and it subsidizes hostels for people with schizophrenia who have been discharged from hospital. MIND also has a publications list, and can provide you with legal and welfare rights advice.

SANE stands for 'Schizophrenia: A National Emergency', a recently formed charity launched with support from News International and the Burton Group. SANE's main goal is to raise funds, both to support research into schizophrenia and to give practical help to whose who are affected by it now. SANE is also sponsoring a major campaign to raise awareness of the problems associated with schizophrenia, spearheaded by *Sunday Times* journalist Marjorie Wallace, who serves as a trustee and as Communications Director of the organization.

The Schizophrenia Association exists to promote a certain view of schizophrenia as a biological condition caused by dietary factors. It is not primarily a support system for relatives of people with schizophrenia, as is the much larger Schizophrenia Fellowship. In its favour, however, it has campaigned actively since the 1960s for a biological, rather than psychological (*see Chapter 3*) view of schizophrenia. In the 1960s biological theories of schizophrenia were not popular, whereas now they are, and it is to its credit that the Schizophrenia Association has been proved right – in general, though not in the precise dietary solution it has promoted. The Schizophrenia Association is known mainly through its sponsorship of conferences on biological aspects of schizophrenia, but its officers will be happy to give you advice on any aspect of the condition.

The Richmond Fellowship is a charitable body which exists to provide hostels for people who have recently been discharged from a psychiatric hospital. It is not politically biased and holds no theoretical view on the nature of schizophrenia. Usually, the social worker in the team of a consultant psychiatrist will approach the organization to place someone who has schizophrenia, but relatives can also apply themselves. It is a very caring organization which understands the problems of the illness and the need for housing for people with schizophrenia who are alienated from their families.

Other Organizations

There are other bodies that are not specifically concerned with the care of people with schizophrenia but which may help you with particular practical problems, such as housing, after-care and legal issues.

The UK Government's housing policy for single, financially deprived people is rudimentary, but they do provide grants to housing associations specifically set up for this purpose. The system varies from town to town, and from borough to borough, and you should seek advice on this. In London, for example, you can contact the Carr-Gomm Society or the Mental After Care Association (*see Appendix B for addresses and telephone numbers*). The chance of an unmarried person with schizophrenia obtaining a council flat is very slim, but these housing organizations may offer not only the possibility of accommodation but a caring and therapeutic atmosphere as well.

After-care is usually organized through the local social services in your borough. They provide day centres where people with schizophrenia can go to obtain company and perform light industrial work in a caring environment. This is usually organized by the social worker who works with the sufferer's consultant psychiatrist, but you can enquire independently at the local branch of your social services department – see your telephone directory for details of your nearest branch.

Finally, if you feel particularly aggrieved over some aspect of care you can approach the Mental Health Act Commission or the Law Society through one of their regional offices, or your local branch of the Citizen's Advice Bureau. The Mental Health Act Commission should be contacted if the issue concerns compulsory admission to hospital (*see Appendix B*). The Law Society can be contacted if you have any other legal problem (*see Appendix B*). The local branch of the Citizen's Advice Bureau, the address of which is to be found in your telephone directory, may be able to help you with practical financial matters such as Social Security payments. I am constantly appalled at how often people with schizophrenia and their relatives fail to take advantage of Sickness Benefit and other payments. I try to encourage sufferers and their families to look into their rights in these matters, but the staff at a Citizen's Advice Bureau are probably the most knowledgeable in this area.

Other organizations that may be helpful are listed in Appendix B. Many are outside the official psychiatric and social services sector, but it may well be worth considering them, depending on the particular problems that you and the person with schizophrenia have.

'There's just something I'd like to ask...'
I hope that the two parts of this chapter – coping with the ups and downs of the comparatively well person who has schizophrenia on a day-to-day basis, and showing you how to

get the best out of the system – have resolved many of your questions. The condition of schizophrenia often baffles both the sufferer and his or her family and friends, but I hope that this book has clarified some of the mysteries. The final chapter includes some of the questions that are commonly asked, either by people with schizophrenia or, more often, by their relatives and friends, some of which may not have been covered in earlier chapters as topics in their own right.

8

COMMON QUESTIONS ABOUT SCHIZOPHRENIA

Most relatives and friends of someone with schizophrenia will have many questions to put to the psychiatrist once the diagnosis has been established. It tends at this stage to be the friends and family who put the questions, for, by the nature of the illness, the sufferer is often unable to ask coherent questions. However, once the person has recovered from the acute stage of the illness and returned to reality, he or she is often very curious about what has happened and about how the future may be affected.

I have tried, so far, to deal systematically with the issues surrounding schizophrenia – its nature, cause, treatment and day-to-day management. Some of the problems that crop up, however, and some of the questions that are frequently asked cannot be covered in this way. For this reason I have included in this chapter questions concerning miscellaneous issues.

Is schizophrenia preventable?
As the precise cause of schizophrenia is still unknown, it is not really possible to talk about prevention. The genetic and environmental causal factors discussed in Chapter 5 are not really avoidable. Even if all people with a definite family history of

schizophrenia were to agree to remain childless, this would not make much difference because schizophrenia can quite often occur in a family with no previous history of it. The possible environmental causes (a complicated birth and a viral infection in the mother in late pregnancy) are not avoidable either, because while good obstetric care may reduce the number of infant deaths and the likelihood of severe mental handicap, it has little effect on the frequency of minor degrees of brain damage.

Preventative measures may eventually come, but they will have to wait until much more is known about schizophrenia. Future developments in genetics, for example, may pave the way for prenatal and pre-pregnancy testing.

Is being in hospital bad for someone with schizophrenia?
Being in hospital for a short while isn't detrimental to anyone. Certainly, it causes a disruption to one's life, and may upset the rest of the family. Some people may hate the rules that apply there – and the food, too. But hospitals are not in themselves damaging places, as some sociologists in the 1960s made them out to be.

The very first episode of a psychotic illness such as schizophrenia should be treated in hospital, as it is crucial to make the correct diagnosis at this stage. Subsequent relapses can be managed outside hospital, if they are not severe. Many people with schizophrenia, however, will refuse to come into hospital either because they think that there is nothing wrong with them or because they feel so frightened or uneasy in the world, due to their disordered perception, that they clutch at the few remaining familiar straws, namely home. The risks they run, through irrational behaviour towards themselves or others, are sometimes so great, however, that immediate hospital admission for any relapse is, in my view, the best course.

The question a relative should ask is not 'Is it a good idea for them to be admitted?' but 'Is it safe for them *not* to be admitted?' For the period of their psychosis, hospital is undoubtedly a more secure place than home, with nurses and doctors and other professionals able to keep a 24-hour vigil. The reasons and benefits of this are discussed more fully at the end of Chapter 6.

Psychiatric hospitals have acquired a bad reputation throughout the world. It is thought that they discourage improvement and contribute to the deterioration in personality of the patients by a process known as 'institutionalization'. Some American sociologists in the 1960s compared them with prisons and even concentration camps. Although some hospitals may have been mismanaged and may have had incompetent staff, to generalize this to all hospitals is very misguided. An institution is no better or worse than its administrators and staff want it to be. Before the 1950s schizophrenia was incurable, and the attitudes within a hospital reflected this. The pessimistic views that then applied to the condition itself, when people with schizophrenia had to be looked after in hospital for the rest of their lives, have now been attached to hospital care in general. In other words, 'institutionalization' was blamed for some of the signs and symptoms of the illness itself. This claim is, therefore, quite unwarranted. The converse of this, namely that 'community care' is the only humane answer, has become an excuse for sloppy diagnosis and treatment. (This, too, is mentioned at the end of Chapter 6.)

Are there pointers to a good or bad outcome?
It is very difficult to predict which people will become the unlucky minority who are left with the social disadvantages discussed in the first part of Chapter 7, despite regular medication. It is equally hard to say who will be the lucky

minority who have only one episode despite being off medication altogether.

There have been many studies of this problem, each of them coming up with a different set of predictors. The only two which regularly appear in all these studies are: (1) whether the person is taking regular medication (= good outcome); and (2) the length of time between the first appearance of the symptoms and the commencement of regular treatment (the longer the delay = the worse the outcome).

The first pointer needs no more clarification. It is the reason why I have stressed throughout the book the crucial importance of correct diagnosis and regular treatment. The second pointer is not so simple. It may mean that if you diagnose the illness at an early stage and treat it effectively then the person has a better outlook. However, it may be that the type of schizophrenia that has a gradual onset (like the illness of Jonathan in Chapter 3), which makes it difficult to diagnose for months or years, has a poor outlook whether it is treated early or late. This is an important issue which is being investigated by psychiatrists at this moment. If the first explanation turns out to be true, that any delay in starting treatment is bad whatever type of schizophrenia it is, this will have a major effect on psychiatric practice.

Are there any warning signs of a relapse?
There are definite warning signs before the sufferer becomes so deluded or hallucinated that you cannot get through to him or her. The signs differ from person to person, and both the sufferer and relatives will get to know them. In most cases the relapse is caused by the sufferer stopping medication, secretly or openly.

I can often tell if patients are relapsing even before I have talked to them, if they are people I have got to know well.

There is something about their general appearance and their mood that gives it away. Like many things about schizophrenia, however, whether from the sufferer's or the observer's point of view, it is difficult to put these subtle changes into words. Sufferers may feel their thoughts slipping away or strange thoughts jostling with familiar ones. The world may begin to seem odd again, eerie or frightening. As a relative you may come to recognize the subtle changes in appearance and mood better than the psychiatrist, who sees the person only every one or two months in the outpatients' clinic. It is a sense that the sufferer is becoming cut-off from the world that probably describes these intuitive feelings best.

Jason, for example, would stop watching television and start reading the dictionary when his relapse was brewing. You might think that reading a dictionary is perfectly acceptable and perhaps to be encouraged, but with Jason it was a sure sign that he had surreptitiously stopped his tablets a few months earlier and was now heading for a major psychotic breakdown.

Bronwyn, another patient, would stop attending her Jehovah's Witness meetings without giving a reason, but I knew, because she would tell me later when she had recovered, that she did it because she felt the other members of the congregation were staring at her in an odd way.

For each person there will usually be a characteristic sign, whether in behaviour, mood, appearance or even tone of voice. Mabel, as another example, would begin talking with a more upper-class – or as her son said, 'high falutin' – accent when her relapse had started.

Is schizophrenia a life-long illness, or is it curable?
In most cases schizophrenia is a life-long condition. The only exception is a small number of people who have only one

episode throughout their entire lives without any need for medication. This is why on page 137 I stated that the crucial factor in how long medication must be taken is whether the person has had two episodes or more within a relatively short period of time. In such cases the chance of further illness is almost certain without medication, and the person's condition *is* life-long.

However, just because an illness cannot be cured once and for all by a single course of treatment it should not be regarded as a tragedy. There are many illnesses that used to cause suffering and death to many but which are now easily controlled by daily medication or monthly injections. Hormonal imbalance due to thyroid disease, and diabetes, for example, were fatal in the 19th century (and earlier this century as well) before thyroid replacement and insulin were manufactured. The underlying illness does not go away, but its effects are completely reversed in the case of thyroid disease and almost completely reversed in the case of diabetes by replacement or insulin therapy respectively.

Schizophrenia should be seen in the same light. Yes, it is life-long, but it is controllable or its effects are mostly reversed by medication.

Are there different types of schizophrenia?
In a word, no, but you may come across a number of different terms, as I shall explain. Emil Kraepelin and Eugen Bleuler, the two psychiatrists at the turn of the century who first identified the illness, believed that there were four types of schizophrenia – paranoid, hebephrenic, catatonic and simple. This classification was based on the different clusters of symptoms that they observed in sufferers. Paranoid schizophrenics had mainly delusions and hallucinations. In the hebephrenic variety it was the disordered way in which emotions and thoughts

were expressed that was most striking. In catatonia the expression of movement and posture was what stood out. In simple schizophrenia the social and personality change (outlined in the first part of Chapter 7) occurred without much in the way of delusions, hallucinations or disordered expression of thoughts, movements and emotions. Some psychiatrists still use these terms but, as most sufferers have a combination of all four, they are not much use in practice.

Some psychiatrists use the terms positive symptoms (delusions and hallucinations) and negative symptoms (apathy, emotional flattening) and call sufferers with the former Type 1 and those with the latter Type 2 schizophrenics. These classifications are arbitrary and of little help to psychiatrist, sufferer or relative.

Are there any tests — biochemical (on blood or urine), psychological or other — that can pick up schizophrenia or a tendency to it in someone as yet unaffected by the condition?
The answer to this is a clear-cut no. There are no biological or psychological tests of schizophrenia even in those who are acutely psychotic — at the height of their illness — so a definitive test of who *might* become psychotic in the future does not yet exist.

Some psychiatrists have claimed that a disorder of attention can be found in the otherwise normal relatives of people with schizophrenia. They base their claim on a study of the errors made during a 'vigilance task'. This type of testing involves something similar to what a radar operator does: watching a screen for irregular blips which might be nearby ships or might be miscellaneous objects, and identifying each one.

Other psychiatrists have looked for shared chromosome types or blood groups, similar to the genetic printing done in criminal cases. Preliminary research indicates that the gene for

schizophrenia could be on chromosome 5 (*see Chapter 5*); however, it is not yet possible either to draw definitive conclusions
or, for that reason, to develop biochemical tests.

There are some ethical problems in identifying a definite
future illness in someone who is now well. People may not
want to know if they will develop a disease. They may prefer
to remain in blissful ignorance. This is true for a disease called
Huntington's chorea, which leads to dementia in late middle
age. If you have a parent with this, you stand a 50 per cent
chance of inheriting the disease. You can take a test in your
twenties or thirties that will predict fairly accurately whether
you will develop the illness or not. Many relatives refuse the
test, and I envisage that the same would be true of relatives of
people with schizophrenia if a similar test were available. The
only difference is that in the case of Huntington's chorea there
is no effective treatment, whereas in schizophrenia there is, so
a prospective test might be more of an advantage in the latter
case.

What future developments are there likely to be?

It is likely that there will be further progress by the end of the
century in two areas – understanding the cause of schizophrenia and improving the available treatments.

In recent years the main development in the search for a
cause has come from the use of brain scans, which can give a
picture of the brain. A straight X-ray of the head will only pick
up bone or air, and until the mid-1970s, in order to investigate
any abnormality of the brain the radiologist had to inject a
radio-opaque dye into an artery, which could be dangerous, or
air into the space surrounding the brain, which was painful.
Now you can take a series of pictures of the brain without danger or pain. It may involve, sometimes, a single injection into
a vein in the arm (the substance injected enhances the result of

the scan), but this is no worse than having a specimen of blood taken.

There are three sorts of brain scans. The simplest is known as computed tomographic scanning (CT scanning). No injection is needed and the subject just has to keep his or her head still for up to half an hour while pictures are taken from various angles by the machine. The resulting picture is clear enough for the radiologist to be able to say whether the surface of the brain is shrunken and whether the ventricles (the cavities within the brain containing fluid) are enlarged, suggesting brain damage.

A much finer picture is given by the newly developed magnetic resonance imaging (MRI). Again, no injection is needed because the machine is in the form of a giant magnet which picks up the electromagnetic forces of all different parts of the brain and produces a picture which is so accurate and detailed that you can see all the major parts of the brain and any abnormalities down to the size of a pea. The only practical problem is that the patient has not only to lie still for about half an hour but has to lie encased in a big tin, which some find claustrophobic.

The third brain scan is known as positron emission tomography (PET), or single photon emission computed tomography (SPECT). The second is a less sophisticated version of the first. Their purpose is to show up any abnormal distribution of blood flow in the brain. A mildly radioactive substance is injected into a vein in the arm, and its course in the brain tracked. This is quite safe provided that no more than two scans are done in any 12-month period.

None of these scans is at the moment of much clinical benefit to an individual sufferer. They are research tools which should, over the next decade, shed considerable light on the cause of schizophrenia.

Advances in treatment are happening all the time. Each new family of antischizophrenic drugs which is brought in is generally freer of side-effects than its predecessors. The latest drugs, clozapine and risperidone, are particularly good in this respect, and there is every reason to suppose that future compounds will be even better.

Are people with schizophrenia violent either to themselves or to others?

Most people who have schizophrenia are never violent at any stage of their illness. A minority are violent while they are acutely psychotic. In between the acute phases of the illness people with schizophrenia are, if anything, less aggressive than normal people.

A few people at the height of their schizophrenic illness are likely to be violent because of their hallucinations and delusions – particularly their delusions. In a study of people with schizophrenia awaiting trial in prison for crimes of violence, Dr Pamela Taylor found that delusions were by far the usual cause of violence. For example, one man had driven a stolen bus at a policeman, missed him and smashed up two cars. He said that he had done this on purpose because the drivers were 'two lefties, so I crunched them on the right wing with the left wing of my bus to show them what buses can do'.

The lesson to be learned from this is that any recurrence of the psychosis, due, as it nearly always is, to stopping medication, should be regarded as a serious matter and the sufferer's psychiatrist contacted with regard to admission.

Violence is sometimes directed not against others but against the self. People with schizophrenia who attempt or actually commit suicide are usually those with a recurrence of their illness after stopping medication.

Are people with schizophrenia responsible for what they do?

This is a question that comes up mainly in the courts, but also affects how you, as a relative, regard lapses into violent or antisocial behaviour. Can you forgive and forget, knowing that it is not really the person whom you know and love who is behind it? Or should you treat it as intentional naughtiness, a premeditated act, and let it affect your opinion of him or her as a person? In simple terms, is he or she mad or bad?

This is a difficult issue. It depends on what he or she did, whether he or she was clearly psychotic at the time, and what he or she was like before the illness. It is best to illustrate the problem with three individual cases, as it cannot be answered in a general way.

Nigel was a young man of 23 and quite normal until his first episode of schizophrenia, when he attacked his mother. He was taken to prison and by the time I saw him had been treated with an antischizophrenic drug for three weeks by the prison psychiatrist. He was then quite normal, but remembered believing his mother was a witch and for this reason hitting her. His mother has since refused to see him ever again, but in fact he has been quite well and reasonably compliant about taking his medication. When Nigel came to trial, the judge nearly sent him permanently to a hospital for the criminally insane on the recommendations of the prison psychiatrist. She said that he had 'lingering delusions' which could make him attack someone again. I objected to this, and the judge agreed to free him with the proviso that he continue to see me and accept treatment.

Nigel was clearly not responsible for what he did

because he was undoubtedly deluded at the time the assault took place. He was a normal law-abiding person before and after his acute illness, and the behaviour was directly attributable to his delusions.

The nature of Brian's antisocial behaviour was harder to establish. He was referred to me for a second opinion as his father was convinced that Brian had schizophrenia, whereas his local psychiatrist thought that he was manic. He had neither delusions nor hallucinations but had signs of formal thought disorder, catatonia and disordered emotional expression. I agreed with his father about the diagnosis. In the ward Brian irritated the nurses and other patients by interfering with all the electrical appliances. He removed the fuse from the plug of the television and no one could understand why the television didn't work until he brought it back a day later. He altered the adjustment on a screw on a motorbike belonging to one of the nurses, and she kept stalling in traffic jams and could not understand why until he admitted what he had done. Most of the staff considered him responsible for these actions and wanted me to discharge him. I felt on balance, however, that his preoccupation with appliances and machines was part of his illness, similar to the unusual interests that I described in other sufferers in Chapter 1 – for example, chimneys – and in Chapter 7.

I did not, therefore, believe that Brian was responsible for this type of behaviour. However, it would have been difficult to prove this in a court of law, if, for example, the nurse had had a serious accident on her bike because of his meddling.

Winston, however, almost certainly knew what he was doing in the following incident. He had walked into a picture shop, ordered a picture which he asked to be framed, paid by cheque and then offered to return a day later to collect the item. In the mean time the owner of the shop noticed something suspicious about the cheque and informed the police, who discovered it had been stolen. When Winston returned to collect his picture a detective was waiting and he was arrested.

Two weeks previously he had attended our casualty department, where he was noted to be psychotic with delusions and hallucinations. He was given a three-week supply of antischizophrenic medication and an appointment to see me in the outpatients' clinic, which was by now a week after the picture incident. When I saw him he was still psychotic, he had not taken his medication and I admitted him directly to hospital where we established a diagnosis of schizophrenia. At his trial, which was mainly for a series of burglaries committed before the psychotic episode as well as for the fraud charge, Winston was quite well; a jury found him guilty of attempted deception and he was sent to prison. Winston was psychotic both before and after the attempted deception at the picture shop and was probably so during the attempted crime. This evidence did not sway the jury, however.

The jury was probably right to think that Winston was responsible for the deception, even though there was good reason to believe he may have been psychotic at the time of the incident. In the first place, the behaviour had very little to do with the content of his delusions and hallucinations; in the second place, although the jury were not told this, he had been a petty criminal for years, long before his illness began. His psychosis, then, was considered not to be related to his criminal activities and it was ruled that he was, in fact, responsible for his actions.

So, responsibility for antisocial acts committed by someone with schizophrenia has to be judged individually. Each case has to be decided on its own merits.

What about sexual behaviour and schizophrenia?
Because schizophrenia frequently affects the ability to initiate and maintain social relationships, this affects sufferers' sexual relationships, as these are the most intimate form of social relationships. Some people with schizophrenia have a low sex drive. Others have a normal or high sex drive but cannot direct it into socially appropriate channels, because they are not married or do not have a regular partner, or do not have the skills to attract others. For this reason they may indulge in open masturbation, or may pester people they are attracted to, or they may become promiscuous.

Their sexually inappropriate behaviour, if it occurs, is part of a wider problem of an inability to conform to social norms.

What about having children?
Some people with schizophrenia, once recovered, naturally enquire whether or not it is 'safe' for them to have children in the future. There are two chief aspects of the problem to be

considered: first, what may be the outcome for the child? Secondly, is it safe for the sufferer?

First, the child has a 1 in 10 chance of developing schizophrenia, which is 10 times the risk to most of us. And, although there is no definite proof that antischizophrenic medication damages the foetus, there is no definite proof that it doesn't.

The tragic consequences of thalidomide have made everyone wary of any drug used in psychiatry. So, for example, thalidomide, which was used to alleviate morning sickness, is now banned. Lithium, the staple and very effective drug for mania, is also harmful to a foetus.

Secondly, as far as someone who has schizophrenia is concerned, if the medication is stopped for the year of trying to conceive and becoming pregnant, the sufferer may relapse. It is not uncommon for a woman to take up to a year to conceive. Looking after a child is very emotionally demanding and, although there is no reason why a woman who has recovered from her illness should be any worse a mother than anyone else, someone who is not completely recovered or who has not appreciated the need for regular medication should be dissuaded from becoming pregnant if at all possible.

The weeks that follow childbirth, known as the *puerperium*, are a particularly vulnerable period in any mother's life as far as psychiatric illness is concerned. A rare condition known as *puerperal psychosis* may occur in the first two weeks, postnatal depression (depression after birth) may develop in the first three to six months, and almost half of the women who have just given birth experience a short-lived period (three days or so) of the miseries, known as 'baby blues'.

Puerperal psychosis, however, is nothing to do with schizophrenia, although it may be misdiagnosed as such. One of the world experts on puerperal psychosis, Professor Robert

Kendell in Edinburgh, has shown convincingly that it is an affective psychosis (*see Chapter 2*). He has also shown that people with schizophrenia have no greater chance of recurrence during the puerperium than at any other time, and women who have had a puerperal psychosis have no greater chance of developing schizophrenia outside the puerperal period than anyone else. Postnatal depression occurs in as many as 1 in 10 women who have recently given birth. It can affect anyone, with or without schizophrenia, and is usually a response to a mother's failure to bond with her child, itself a consequence of a deprived childhood on her own part or her current interpersonal difficulties. 'Baby blues' is a hormonal-induced mood change, which again has nothing to do with schizophrenia.

Although these three conditions – puerperal psychosis, postnatal depression and 'baby blues' – are unrelated to schizophrenia, they are a source of potential stress to someone with schizophrenia who gives birth. Coupled with the stress of pregnancy and the increased risk of schizophrenia in the child, I believe that they make childbearing for someone with schizophrenia a very hazardous matter.

How can you tell the difference between hallucinations caused by illegal drugs and hallucinations caused by schizophrenia?
At first you cannot, and this is one of the reasons why it is desirable to admit to hospital someone thought to have schizophrenia for the first time. The age at which schizophrenia typically starts, particularly in young men, coincides with the age at which adolescents may start experimenting with illegal drugs. Some of these drugs, notably LSD ('acid'), amphetamines ('speed') and cannabis ('dope', 'hashish'), can induce very powerful hallucinations. You will see that I touched on this in Chapter 2, in the section on Delirium, and in Chapter 7, in the section entitled Addictions. Once the person is

admitted to hospital, he or she can be observed for several days while taking no drugs at all. Simple urine and blood tests can be done to establish the presence of any hallucinogenic drug in the body, and, if it exists, to monitor its decreasing level. Once the body is free of the drug, the hallucinations should cease if they have been induced by the drug rather than a mental illness. If they continue, it is reasonably safe to assume that the hallucinations have been caused by a mental illness, such as schizophrenia.

Do people with schizophrenia have a split personality?

Psychiatrists tend to dismiss this common question as naïve, and are at pains to explain that schizophrenia is nothing like the lay-person's image of a split personality, who can be all sweetness one minute and ferocious the next, a Jekyll and Hyde character. I think, on the other hand, that people with schizophrenia *do* have a split personality, but it is different from the popular concept of a split personality fostered by films.

People with schizophrenia are not simply prone to have two opposing temperaments, but *many*. The split is more like a multiple fracture than a clean break. Moreover, the split is more radical than is suggested in the Jekyll and Hyde analogy, because it affects the way perceptions, thoughts, emotions and actions are all linked. Dr Jekyll was a caring doctor with high moral beliefs and sensitive feelings. Mr Hyde was an evil criminal, angry and with no feelings for his fellow humans. Each personality was fully formed and there was complete consistency among its parts. In schizophrenia, moods, ideas and actions may change dramatically from moment to moment, but it is very rare that there are distinct personality types to be recognized. It is better to regard the result as a *shattered* rather than as a split personality.

The ideas I discussed in Chapter 5 concerning the possible causes of schizophrenia also suggest that there is a split between different parts of the same mental function and between different sides of the brain. However, the result is, as mentioned above, more in the nature of a shattered rather than a split mind, because overall control has been lost. It is not just that one set of functions temporarily replaces another. Each set of functions is working away, trying to make the best of the chaos reigning in another part of the mind.

Is there any advantage in having schizophrenia?

Schizophrenia is usually viewed by professionals and lay-people alike as a dreadful tragedy in a family. There was a brief period in the 1960s, however, when certain maverick psychiatrists in Britain and some sociologists in North America tried to turn this attitude on its head and to show that schizophrenia is more real and true than real life itself. Was there anything in this? And does having had schizophrenia confer some insight into life?

The answer in both cases, in my view, is no. Ronald (R. D.) Laing was the main instigator in Britain of a view that schizophrenia was not a real disease, but merely a reaction on the part of someone, usually the weakest in a family, to stresses and strains within the family. According to Laing, the stronger family members colluded with the psychiatrist to label one member as schizophrenic and so solve all the problems of the entire family. The person so labelled then benefited from this experience, so the story went, and emerged as stronger and more mature than before. This idea is rubbish, as Laing himself was later to admit. To have schizophrenia is to be alienated from society; in that sense Laing was right. But this alienation is neither a consciously chosen way of dealing with troublesome relatives, nor is it a step on the way to maturity.

In the early stage of schizophrenia, sufferers may, if they have artistic or literary talent, portray their new existence in such a way that a normal person, who has never experienced or even conceived of a different way of seeing the world, can gain insight into this. The sufferers themselves, when they recover, will appreciate more than normal people how fragile the fabric of existence is. However, they still may not be wiser for it. They may feel more vulnerable, more wary of life. The generation of young people who took hallucinogenic drugs in the 1960s are probably no more emotionally mature than if they hadn't. They may have seen that the mind is a fragile mechanism, but they are not necessarily wiser people as a consequence.

The only people, paradoxically, who might benefit from having had a schizophrenic illness are psychiatrists and other professionals whose job it is to understand what schizophrenia is like. The consequences of the condition, however, would probably make them unreliable as professionals.

Do people with schizophrenia look different from other people?
This may seem a trivial, if not impertinent, question. It is undoubtedly true, however, that many people who have schizophrenia stand out from the rest of us, for a combination of reasons.

Sufferers often look at you in a piercing way, forcing you to look away. Others may not look at you at all. A social psychologist would say that they do not obey the unwritten rules of eye gaze or intimate eye contact. They do not 'respect your space' or, alternatively, do not 'engage' you at all, and this makes you feel uneasy. ('Engage' in this context is a technical term meaning 'engross', 'involve' or 'attract the attention of'.)

They tend to talk *at* you rather than *to* you. This habit is not confined to people with schizophrenia, but they have a general tendency (as I noted in Chapter 1 when I discussed Real Meanings in the section entitled Disturbed Thinking) to disregard the conventions about conversation, and this can be very off-putting.

People with schizophrenia may dress or apply make-up in an unusual way, showing no awareness of which colours go with which and no sense of knowing how to show themselves to best advantage.

Their gestures may seem somewhat out of place and their behaviour in everyday social encounters may take you by surprise. They may sit too close for comfort, for example, or conduct a conversation at an unreasonable distance.

All these characteristics are subtle, and in no way specific to schizophrenia, but taken together they contribute to the unease one often feels in their presence. It is not that they are merely rejecting etiquette in social matters. One senses immediately if a normal adolescent is being surly or if a stranger is being purposely rude. In the case of schizophrenia it is the lack of any consistent social poise or attitude that comes across, combined with a total lack of awareness sufferers have about themselves.

Is schizophrenia contagious?
This is not the trivial question it may seem. Many illnesses of the brain (such as meningitis and viral encephalitis) are infections transmitted from one person to another. The most common route is by what is known as droplet spread – the moisture drops emitted by an infected person's coughing or sneezing travel to other people and infect them. This accounts for the spread of both meningitis (an infection of the covering of the brain) and encephalitis (an infection of the substance of the brain itself). AIDS and syphilis, both of which are illnesses that affect the brain, are caught through transmission of

body fluids, such as blood and semen, from one person to another.

There is no evidence at all that you can catch schizophrenia in any of these ways from an affected person. If it were infectious by droplet spread, psychiatrists and psychiatric nurses would have a much higher rate of schizophrenia than average, but this is not the case.

The only link with an infectious agent is the finding that people who develop schizophrenia are slightly more likely to have been born in the winter months (*see page 107*), but this points to foetal brain damage caused by a viral infection carried by their mother during the pregnancy. One cannot rightly say that the foetus 'catches schizophrenia' this way, only that it sustains a particular sort of brain damage that predisposes the person to schizophrenia in late adolescence. The virus does not remain inside waiting to infect someone else. The viral damage, if it occurs, is over and done with before the person is born; he or she then ceases to be infectious.

There is no specific schizophrenia-inducing virus. It is the part of the brain that the virus attacks, not the particular virus, that is the crucial factor.

Are people with schizophrenia more at risk of developing certain physical illnesses?

Once people have developed schizophrenia they are no more likely than anyone else to fall ill with a physical condition unconnected with the side-effects of their medication.

Certain physical illnesses that affect the brain such as epilepsy, stroke and rare metabolic and inflammatory diseases can, in the way mentioned in Chapter 4, lead on to schizophrenia at a much later date. But these illnesses come before the schizophrenia, not after it.

There is one physical illness, rheumatoid arthritis, which

some experts believe is *less* common in people with schizophrenia than in those without the illness, but the evidence for this is not strong. The same reduced risk has been claimed for cancer, but the case for this is also shaky: it is also surprising since a very high proportion of people with schizophrenia are heavy smokers.

Should people with schizophrenia be allowed to drive?
In my view there is no reason why not, provided that they are comparatively well, and taking medication. There are rules about driving public vehicles – taxis, buses, trains – which may render them ineligible for this sort of work. One of my patients used to be a taxi-driver but has now been told that he cannot reapply for his licence because he is on medication. This may seem unfair, but the only answer is to apply to the licensing body and see what they say. In fact, the former taxi-driver keeps stopping his medication in the hope that he will remain well, but, unfortunately, he then relapses.

Can someone with schizophrenia get life insurance?
Life insurance companies will exact a higher premium if they know that the person who is applying for insurance has had a schizophrenic breakdown, but they will not turn down the application outright. If there are any problems you should involve the person's psychiatrist in correspondence with the company.

Has schizophrenia always existed throughout the ages – or is it a modern disease?
This is not very relevant to the quality of life of someone suffering from schizophrenia, but it is an intriguing question nevertheless. It is probable that schizophrenia has always been around, but unrecognized, and called by whatever was the

fashionable label for outsiders or alienated people at the time. In the late Middle Ages sufferers from schizophrenia may have been branded as witches, for example.

There are some psychiatrists who regard schizophrenia as a modern disease. Some of them see it as a reaction to a modern and developed industrialized society, others as an epidemic which originated in Europe at the beginning of the 19th century and swept across the world. Neither of these views has much support. Diseases of diverse kinds have a historical ebb and flow, regardless of the introduction of effective treatment, and it may be that schizophrenia was relatively uncommon before the 19th century. Some authorities are now claiming that, regardless of the advances in treatment, it is on the wane in the latter part of the 20th century. I have considerable doubts about any of these claims, as psychiatric records were poor before the 19th century and the condition occurs to the same extent in all countries, developed or underdeveloped.

FURTHER READING

Jacqueline M. Atkinson, *Coping with Schizophrenia: A Guide to What it Is and What Can Be Done to Help* (Thorsons, 1989)

——, *Schizophrenia: A Guide for Sufferers and their Families* (Turnstone, 1985)

Andrew Croyden Smith, *Schizophrenia and Madness* (George Allen & Unwin, 1982)

Nona Dearth, Barbara J. Labenski, M. Elizabeth Mott and Lillian M. Pellegrini, *Families Helping Families* (Penguin, 1986)

Anne Deveson, *Tell Me I'm Here* (Penguin, 1992)

E. Fuller Torrey, *Schizophrenia and Civilization* (NY: Jason Aronson, 1980)

——, *Surviving Schizophrenia: A Family Manual* (NY: Harper & Row, rev. edn, 1988)

Clare Greer and John Wing, *Schizophrenia at Home: The Impact of Schizophrenia on Family Life, and How Relatives Cope* (National Schizophrenia Fellowship, 1988)

Gwen Howe, *The Reality of Schizophrenia* (Faber & Faber, 1991)

—, *Schizophrenia: A Fresh Approach* (David & Charles, 1986)

Steven Jones and Frank Tallis, *Coping with Schizophrenia* (Sheldon Press, 1994)

Brenda Lintner, *Living with Schizophrenia: A Guide for Patients and Relatives* (Macdonald & Co, 1989)

M. Moate and D. Enoch, *Schizophrenia: Voices in the Dark* (Kingsway Publications, 1990)

National Schizophrenia Fellowship, *Living with Schizophrenia: By the Relatives* (National Schizophrenia Fellowship, undated)

Seeman, Littman *et al.*, *Living and Working with Schizophrenia: Information and Support for Patients and their Families, Friends, Employers and Teachers* (The Open University Press, 1982)

Marjorie Wallace, *The Forgotten Illness* (Times Newspapers, London, 1987; part of *The Times* campaign on schizophrenia. Available from the National Schizophrenia Fellowship or from SANE — see *Appendix B*).

USEFUL ADDRESSES

UK

NATIONAL ORGANIZATIONS
National Schizophrenia Fellowship
28 Castle Street
Kingston upon Thames
Surrey KT1 1SS
Tel: 0181–547 3937

MIND – National Association for Mental Health
Granta House
15–19 Broadway
London E15 4BQ
Tel: 0181–519 2122

SANE (Schizophrenia: A National Emergency)
2nd Floor
199–205 Old Marylebone Road
London NW1 5QP
Tel: 0171–724 6520 (admin)

Helpline: 0171–724 8000 (within London)
0345–678000 (from elsewhere in the UK; calls
are charged at the local rate)

Schizophrenia Association
Bryn Hyfryd
The Crescent
Bangor
Gwynedd LL57 2AG
Tel: 01248 354048

Richmond Fellowship
8 Addison Road
Kensington
London W14 8BL
Tel: 0171–603 6373

HELP WITH LEGAL OR HOUSING ISSUES
Carr-Gomm Society
Telegraph Hill Centre
Kitto Road
London SE14 5TY
Tel: 0171–277 6060

The Mental After Care Association
25 Bedford Square
London WC1B 3HW
Tel: 0171–436 6194

Mental Health Act Commission
Maid Marian House
56 Houndsgate
Nottingham NG1 6BG
Tel: 0115 950 4040
(They can give you the address of regional offices.)

The Law Society
113 Chancery Lane
London WC2A 1PL
Tel: 0171–242 1222
*(from whom you can obtain the address of your local Law
Society office)*

OTHER SOURCES OF SUPPORT

Carers National Association
20–25 Glass House Yard
London EC1A 4JS
Tel: 0171–490 8818
*This provides practical information and contacts with other people in your
situation.*

*The Association of Community Health Councils for England
and Wales*
30 Drayton Park
London N5 1PB
Tel: 0171–609 8405
*This is the consumers' watchdog in the NHS and provides information on local
services. You can contact the central body or try your local branch, listed in the
telephone book.*

The Ex-Services Mental Welfare Society
Broadway House
2nd Floor
The Broadway
Wimbledon
London SW19 1RL
Tel: 0181–543 6333

This has charitable funds for ex-soldiers, -airmen, -sailors and their families in financial difficulty due to mental illness in one of their members.

The Health Service Commissioner for England
11th floor
Mill Bank Tower
Mill Bank
London SW1T 4QP
Tel: 0171–276 2035

This is your final resort if you have obtained no satisfaction locally about your grievances. This is the office of the Ombudsman who will take your complaint seriously and at the highest level. You should use this only if you find that complaining at a local level first to your psychiatrist and then to the Community Health Council is to no avail.

The Holiday Care Service
2 Old Bank Chambers
Station Road
Horley
Surrey RH6 9HW
Tel: 01293 774535

This organization provides information about the possibility of subsidized holidays for carers and sufferers alike.

The Jewish Welfare Board
221 Golders Green Road
London NW11 9DQ
Tel: 0181–458 3282

Many ethnic minorities have their own welfare system; this one gives information and may provide finance for hostel accommodation for people of Jewish origin who have schizophrenia.

Remploy
415 Edgware Road
Cricklewood
London NW2 6LR
Tel: 0181–235 0500

This organization provides sheltered employment for disabled people.

The Simon Community
P.O. Box 1187
London NW5
Tel: 0171–485 6639

This organization owns hostels mainly for single homeless men but is supportive towards anyone who has had a psychiatric breakdown.

The Women's Royal Voluntary Service
234–244 Stockwell Road
London SW9 9SP
Tel: 0171–416 0146

This organization and its various local branches (listed in your telephone directory) has its own meals on wheels service.

USA and Canada

The American Schizophrenia Association
c/o Huxley Institute
114 First Avenue
New York, NY 10021

The Canadian Schizophrenia Foundation
2229 Broad Street
Regina
Saskatchewan
SP4 1Y7

Australia

There are various fellowships in Australia; most states have them.

Schizophrenia Fellowship of New South Wales
The Secretary
8 Dunmore Avenue
Carlingford
NSW 2118
Tel: 02 88 2053

The World Schizophrenia Fellowship
238 Davenport Road
118 Toronto
Ontario M5R 1J6
Tel: 1 416 960 1808

INDEX